Bonetta Holloway

JUST A GIRL...

A JOURNEY WITH GOD

JUST A GIRL...
A JOURNEY WITH GOD

Copyright © 2022 Bonetta Holloway

ISBN 978-1-946683-48-9
Library of Congress Control Number 2022912265

Rapier Publishing Company
Dothan, Alabama 36301

www.rapierpublishing.com
Facebook: www.rapierpublishing@gmail.com
Twitter: rapierpublishing@rapierpub

Printed in the United States of America
All rights reserved under the International Copyright Law.
Contents and/or cover may not be reproduced in whole or in part in any form without the consent of the Publisher or Author.

Book Cover Design: Daniel Ojedokun
Book Layout: Rapture Graphics
Cover Photo: Shutterstock Photo #312353849 (Enhanced License)

DEDICATION

First and foremost, I want to thank God for inspiring me to write. And then I want to thank my husband for being so supportive of me, and believing in me. He has been excited about this book from day one. Also, I want to thank my children and grandchildren for their support. When I refer to my children, it always includes my daughters-in-law and sons-in-law. We know they have been placed in our family by God and we are thankful for that. They have all been such an encouragement to me, all along this journey. I would like to thank a host of other family and friends that believe in me, and my walk with God.

Finally, I want to thank my husband for the memories of his childhood. My daughter-in-law, Leanna, for sharing some of her writing skills in this book, and Joshua and Leanna's love story. I want to thank my daughter, Rebekah, for sharing her testimony.

THANK YOU!

Just A Girl, A Journey With God

IN LOVING MEMORY

We have all lost loved ones and friends along this journey of life. No matter how many years have stretched out between then and now, it still hurts. I can't name everyone, but I would like to remember my grandparents, my aunt Cindy and Shona, who were taken in a tragic accident when I was "just a girl". Also, my mother and dad, and Phillip's mother and dad. These people were such an inspiration and encouragement so often in our walk with God. And finally, our grandson, Aiden, who we lost on December 20, 2021. I must say it was the most devastating thing we had ever walked through. Aiden was eleven years old. He had autism, epilepsy, and was nonverbal, but he was the sweetest child I had ever met. He faced a lot of physical battles from the time he was eighteen months old until age eleven. I know it was in God's divine plan to take our little superhero home. Even though it broke our hearts, I am thankful he is now whole.

Bonetta Holloway

IN MEMORY OF AIDEN

In 2010, what a blessing God gave to us, our first grandchild, Aiden James Wilson. We were beyond excited. He was so tiny, weighing only 6 pounds. His timy hands big enough to wrap around our hearts, and he held on tightly. We didn't realize it then, but from the moment this little Wilson baby took his first breath, he had superpowers, and as he grew, we began to see its effect.

His favorite superhero was Captain America. I guess we never realized it before, but these two superheroes had something in common. Captain America had the ability to move very quickly, and so did Aiden. His eye coordination was right on spot. When he saw someone who needed to be rescued from their burdens, he would move quickly to get to them. He, of course, would have to catch his parents by surprise and pull away from the firm grip they had on him. He would then run like the wind, until he was face to face with that burdened soul. He would "so gracefully" jump up and down in place, with a smile bigger than Texas; and that is when all their burdens just rolled away.

Yes, his greatest superpower was his smile. Aiden was nonverbal. You see God planned it this way, because he wanted to show the world the power of a smile. I often said he had a million-dollar smile, but then again you can't put a price on a gift from God. I believe Aiden knew that his smile was a gift because he used it so very skillfully.

He couldn't say "I love you," but when he took you by the hand and interlocked his fingers with yours, and then looked at you with that million-dollar smile, he said it more fluently than an

English professor. He didn't like to 'hug or cuddle,' but that was ok; when he smiled at you, so much love radiated from it, that you could feel its caress.

His smile made him more sociable than anyone else. With that superpower alone he could transform a stranger into a friend in a moment of time. All he had to do was walk up to someone with that smile, and they remembered him forever.

Well, it only took eleven years before Aiden said, mission accomplished, and then God took him home. And when he left here on Dec. 20, 2021, he left here still gripping our hearts tightly in his hands.

We are forever grateful to him for the work that he did here. "Aiden James Wilson" will never be forgotten. He will go down in history as a powerful man of God. His mission was to change the world, "HIS WORLD." For anyone who were ever a part of "his world" have been forever changed.

"Aiden" you are LOVED and MISSED

Bonetta Holloway

PREFACE

This is a nonfictional God inspired book. I titled it JUST A GIRL, because that is all I was when God found me, and I started on A JOURNEY WITH GOD....

My desire is that this book will build a faith and a confidence in you towards God. This book is not filled with trauma and pain. Instead, it displays trials, hardships, and victories.

At just thirteen years old I was involved with a man ready for marriage and family. I was headed down a road that no doubt would have brought me much heartache and grief. But GOD in his mercy, sent a detour, and REWROTE MY LIFE. I did get married just before turning fifteen, and ever since then I've been on a journey with God.

I am now a woman; a pastor/ Evangelist wife, a mother of six wonderful children, a mother-in-law to six of the most amazing spouses that my children could have ever found, and a grandmother. I must say my heart is full.

Together, my husband and I so frequently faced hardships, climbed mountains, and crossed valley's. Many times, we were tired and weak, but with the same goal, the same mind, and one heartbeat, we pressed on. And now by God's Grace, forty years later, after the dust has somewhat settle, we are still standing.

Just A Girl, A Journey With God

JUST A GIRL,
A JOURNEY WITH GOD....

THE AUCTION BLOCK

Looking back on my life, I felt as though I was standing beside an auction block. Just waiting my turn, while one by one someone is sold to the highest bidder. I felt like my life had a destination without my consent, because I was only thirteen years old. I was dating a nineteen year old man, who is ready for marriage. Confused to why I was in this situation, and only seeing one bidder at the auction. I was sure my life's destiny was set.

1 | THE WEDDING

The gentle evening breeze blew softly, chasing away the heat of the hot summer day. A nearby dogwood tree surrendered a few small flowers from its blossoming branch, while the wind made the small white petals dance with twirls as they flew past me. They were so white – white like the dress my older sister was wearing now. The delicate cap sleeves falling just over her shoulders; the bodice covered in elegant lace gracefully fell around her waist, puffing up just a bit and skimming her knees. So dainty and elegant she was, standing hand in hand with her handsome, soon-to-be husband. The late summer sun had just begun to set; its golden beams touching the couple, making the whole scene quite radiant for the small country wedding it was. Standing on the front porch that stretched all the way across the old farmhouse where Ronald and his eight siblings were raised, Ronald's Mother, Elaine, was beaming with pride and excitement as friends and family gathered on the front lawn. They were witnesses to this union between two people so in love. Theresa and Ronald ready to embark upon their future, were now standing in front of a minister. Then I heard, "Do you, Ronald, take this woman to be your wife, to love and to hold, till death do you part?" Then he turned to my sister and asked her the same, and they both replied, "I do." This was quite an experience for a little girl to witness. My sister was about to be a married woman.

Grandma's hand gripping a small blue lace handkerchief, reached out and rested it on my shoulder to steady me. As I shifted from one foot to the other. I was awestruck by this gorgeous scene. It had been a long day filled with excitement. Everyone was getting ready for this big day. Finally, I heard, "I now pronounce you man and wife." I let out a sigh as the preacher said, "Ronald you may kiss your bride." The little crowd of people that were gathered on the front lawn cheered. There may have been a few tears. Mom went over and gave Theresa and Ronald a big hug. I could see that she was so proud of them. All I could think of, was one day, when it was my turn to stand with the man I loved, I hoped I would be as beautiful as Theresa on that day. I couldn't imagine how my mom was feeling. Yes, this wedding was over, but in a scant four weeks my oldest sister, Ann, would also be getting married. Two weddings and only a month apart – Theresa in June and Ann in July. Ann was having a beautiful church wedding. Her white lace dress, fitted at the waist, and then layered all the way to the floor. Though I was very happy for them, I felt as though I had been cheated and I should have had them at home with me a bit longer. Sure, I had my four brothers, but it wasn't the same. At nine, my sisters provided a comfort and rock for me. When I was with them, I felt as though nothing could ever harm me. Why did I feel cheated you may ask? Theresa was only fourteen on her wedding day and Ann was sixteen. Most would wonder why any mother would allow her daughters to marry so young. All I can say is that it was a different era then – especially in our neck of the woods. It was common for many girls to marry young. In those days most everyone had large families. The boys helped their fathers. The girls helped their mothers with cooking, cleaning, and taking care their siblings. So, by the time they were teenagers, they were mature enough to take care of a home and a family of their own. So yes, a lot of what you see on 'Little House on the Prairie' is true. Both of my grandmothers were married at the age of thirteen, and my mom was only fifteen on her wedding day.

Just A Girl, A Journey With God

My dad was twenty-five and mom was fifteen. They had only been married 10 months when my oldest brother, Earbie, came along; and then Ann and Theresa right behind him. Mom often talked of the challenges she faced with all three of them being in diapers at once – and disposable diapers were unheard of in those days. My brothers Andy and Kent came next, then it was me. On my first birthday, our baby brother Clifton was born. Mom had seven children in 10 years. She kept the old tradition and raised us the way she was raised. Even with all the stress of raising children, Mom and Dad were happily married for sixty-one years

2| A SUMMER JOB

I am a Louisiana girl. Jambalaya, crawfish pie, and file gumbo were always a must in our home. But Louisiana is not only known for its Cajun cooking. It is also the nursery capital. Louisiana ships millions of plants a year across America. My mother worked in the nurseries for as long as I can remember, and in the summer of 1978 that is where I got my first job.

It was there I met a young man who came by to purchase some plants. He walked over and began to talk to me. Looking a lot older than I was, he asked me out on a date. When I told him I was only thirteen he didn't believe me. My mother was working with me, so he asked her how old I was. She said, yes, she is thirteen, but she is allowed to date. I remember having so many mixed feelings at that moment. I felt young and vulnerable, but apparently my mother didn't see me that way. Part of me wanted to say 'no' and hide, but there was also an excitement. It was a chance to begin a new chapter in my life. I remember seeing my sisters on their wedding days, and the new lives they had started. I was somewhat excited to do the same. So, we did begin to date for a while. At first it was exciting, but what I didn't realize, he was nineen and ready to start thinking about marriage. At first it sounded exciting, but I had some anxiety. The young man was good to me and had a good job, but I was having some doubt. I must admit I was scared. When I tried to talk to mother about the unsure feelings, she reminded me that he was a good man and could provide for me.

Just A Girl, A Journey With God

In the quiet of the night when I was alone, I would wonder 'can this be normal?' How could this be happening to me when in many ways I still felt like a little girl? I did not understand why I was having these feelings of doubt. On the surface it all seemed good, but somehow my heart was telling me differently. These troubling feelings of fear and anxiety were coming from within my heart. Mom and dad were only seeing things from their personal experience.

After enduring the long nights of anxiety over my impending marriage, I wavered between excitement and serious doubt. I realize now that those were nights God was trying to talk to me. But, like Samuel, I did not know the Lord yet. I had no idea that God would be interested in someone like me; that He even cared what happened to me. I only saw one path, so, I would calm myself with the facts. This man cared about me and could provide for me. If I passed up this opportunity, there may not be another.

I think a lot of young people feel the pressure of not getting another chance. Feeling like there is only one path and letting fear and doubt choose life's journey for them.

But that all changed for me one summers evening. As the sun began to lower in that beautiful Louisiana sky, I walked out onto the porch that stretched across the wood frame house that my dad had built. I was quietly sitting in the rocking chair where dad would often retire from a long day of work. Trying, to clear my mind from a busy day, I saw Aunt Cindy pulling in the driveway and rolling down the window. "Come ride with me, Bonetta!" Never passing up a chance to visit with my mom's baby sister, I ran down to her car without a second thought. As I was getting into the car, I said, "Where are we going, Aunt Cindy?"

She said, "Nowhere in particular. I just want to visit with you."

I always admired her peaceful disposition. She was nineteen and single and loved to take time out for her nieces and nephews.

As we began to cruise the streets of that peaceful little town of Turkey Creek, with her sweet calm voice, she said "So, how have you been?" "Good I guess." Still speaking to me gently, she asked "So how are you feeling about marriage?"

It was at that moment that I realized no one had ever asked me that question before. Thinking for a moment and not sure if I should say anything, I stammered. "Well, funny you should ask." Aunt Cindy always seemed to know when I was troubled.

She said, "Bonetta, you know you can always talk to me."

"Well," I said with a bit of a sigh, "during the day, I am fine. But at night when all is quiet, I have these uncertain feelings, almost as if I am in a trap."

Holding my hand, she said "I want you to know that you have been on my mind, and I have been praying for you. You know God loves you, don't you?"

I replied with a rebellious "Yeah, sure." Well, I did not know it, but I didn't want her to know how far away from God I was. As we continued to talk, she encouraged me to wait on marriage.

"You have plenty of time and God has a special purpose for your life and maybe you should focus on that right now."

I was stunned to hear that God would care for someone like me. I had never been a church member, so I didn't know how to pray, but looking back, I now realize that when we talk to God in our hearts, He hears us.

Aunt Cindy explained to me that I wasn't being forced to marry and was much too young to make my own decision about marriage – especially at thirteen! I could not get Aunt Cindy's voice out of my head. Her words ('you know God loves you') kept rolling over and over, and the thought ('why don't you just focus on that right now?') was loud in my Spirit. Well, I didn't exactly know how, but one thing I did know is that God knows who I am, and He loves me.

Now I see another bidder at the auction block, and instead of fear and questions, at just one short glimpse of Him, I see love and compassion – a love greater than I ever knew could exist.

I knew it wouldn't be easy, but I had to end this relationship with this man. I could hear whisperings. "She's making a big mistake. She'll regret it." But I had never felt more at peace with my decision. For the first time I was making my own decisions. I did not become a Christian at this time. But now I know there is a God, and He knows my name.

3 | THE CAR ACCIDENT

I am thankful Aunt Cindy took the time to visit with me that day. She had many nieces and nephews that she loved and would always take the time to care for them. There wasn't a Sunday that went by that she didn't try to get someone to go to church with her.

Cindy's sister-in-law had a beautiful daughter. Her name was Shona. She had just moved down from Ville Platte, Louisiana. Shona was a dear friend of mine. She was 14 years old; she had an olive complexion and dark black hair just below the shoulders. Her face was always radiant with a beautiful smile. Those dark brown eyes were always full of expectancy, and her personality could light up any room. She never had the opportunity to go to church, so she did not know the Lord.

Aunt Cindy invited her to church one Sunday afternoon in February of 1979. Shona went, along with her 10-year-old stepbrother, Shane, and her stepsister, Charlotte, who was eight. That night at church, they had what was described as a wonderful service. The power of God had been manifested, and Shona gave her heart to God. God saved her and filled her with the Holy Ghost. The people who were there at that meeting said she had such a glow on her face and smiled as if the weight of the world had been lifted. That night as Aunt Cindy was driving home, Shona was sitting in the front seat with Cindy and grandma, Shane and Charlotte were in the back seat with Grandpa. They were about ten miles from home when a man who was driving an 18-wheeler while being intoxicated, crossed into their lane, hitting them head on. Everyone in the front seat was instantly killed. The car quickly caught fire and would have also killed everyone in the back seat, but thankfully there were people close by to pull them from the burning vehicle.

The devastating news that Cindy, Grandma, and Shona were killed, and that grandpa, Shane, and Charlotte where badly injured was heartbreaking. We were all in shock – a horrible bad dream! I kept thinking I will wake up and realize it is just a nightmare. Our hearts were broken. Questions running through the minds of everyone – 'What is the purpose for this? What is God doing? How could this be part of God's plan?'

Today many years after the accident that claimed the lives of my dear loved ones, I am reminded of the alabaster box. The alabaster box wasn't broken by accident or because someone was angry, it was broken gracefully. Once it was broken all was given nothing spared.

This woman didn't know that she could give herself to Jesus, so, she gave the most precious thing that she had in her possession, the ointment in an alabaster box. In her willingness to sacrifice such a precious gift, it filled the air with the sweet-smelling ointment that brought healing and restoration to her life. Her gift of the alabaster box was misunderstood even by those closest to Jesus, yet the one to whom it belonged, and the one to whom it was given, understood perfectly. Jesus valued her offering, those around her could only see the empty broken vessel, or waste and poverty, but Jesus saw her heart and she saw grace. Only God can use brokenness to make us strong, and nothing can compare to being gracefully broken.

Aunt Cindy was a wonderful Christian, and though her life was short, the things she accomplished will be everlasting. She forever lives in my memories, and I am who I am today, because she was willing to take the time to encourage me. When I was alone and afraid, she showed me a way out. Don't be afraid to be a servant for God. Always be ready to defend those who are too weak to defend themselves. God needs each one of us to war in His Kingdom.

Grandpa was only given 48 hours to live. All his vital organs were seriously injured. The doctor told the family that he wanted to put him in a nursing home until he passed. The family was not willing to do that and decided to bring him home and take care of him. Aunt Helen and Uncle Bobby opened their house and took him in. They put his hospital bed in the living room, and everyone took turns staying with him. He had to have 24-hour care. So, there were many nights that Aunt Helen and Uncle Bobby slept on the floor in the living room. Uncle David spent much of his time helping, along with all the others pitching in when they could. Grandpa was much loved by his family. He was a wonderful Christian and was always a strong man and hard worker.

Grandpa was a logger by trade and for a hobby, he worked a five-acre garden with a mule. He didn't need to raise that garden every year, but he enjoyed sharing the bounty with his family and the community. As a little girl, I would go stand at the end of that garden in amazement, as grandpa would shout out to ole queen "Hee" and ole Queen would turn to the right, and then later he would call out "Haw" and then she would turn to the left. And then when he came to the end of the turn row, he would say, "Woe

Queen," and Queen would wait until she heard another command. Grandpa was in his late 60's but he walked behind Queen like he was a young man. He had Queen for 15 years. Queen always knew what grandpa wanted her to do. I can remember seeing love in grandpa's actions towards ole Queen, and ole Queen loved grandpa.

Grandpa, a true man of God, was active in his church and loved attending services. After the accident, Uncle David thought it a good idea to have Grandpa's pastor come and hold prayer meetings at Aunt Helen's house, not realizing at the time that it was God's plan all along. Grandpa's pastor, Rev. Dillard Holloway, came once a week on Thursday night. As time went on, Grandpa began to heal. Aunt Helen could see Grandpa improving. About ten months went by and Grandpa started getting up and walking a few steps each day. Grandpa was 68 when the accident happened, up until now he was always strong and healthy. He loved life and began to fight for it. It wasn't long until we all realized God had worked a miracle. Eighteen months after the accident, he was able to move back home and resume his life. I have heard doctors say we don't hold life in our hands, God does. Grandpa was living proof of that. The doctors only gave him 48 hours, but God gave him six more years. Thank You JESUS!

A born-again experience puts you in a bracket of life above death. That doesn't mean you will never die. It simply means it gives you the power to be more than a conquer – power to believe that God can and will do anything we can ask or think, according to the power that works in us. We can proclaim that greater is He that is in me than he that is in the world, and faith makes you a candidate for God's miracles.

Bonetta Holloway

When you are a child of God, you belong to him. He is your Father. Don't ever give up because circumstances tell you to. God always has the last say. So many people stop short of what God has for them because of circumstances. We never know until we try, and we can't win if we don't fight.

4 | THE HOME PRAYER MEETING

The prayer meetings continued about eight months and the crowd grew. Every Thursday night, Aunt Helen's living room would be packed – mostly with Grandpa's children and grandchildren. My mother gave her heart to the Lord in one of those prayer meetings. Week after week, she would invite me to go with her. I really thought she was only attending them because she was still grieving the loss of her family. Every week I made a new excuse to why I could not go. I turned her down so many times until I felt ashamed. It was clear she was not going to stop asking, so, finally, I said, "I will go with you one time, if you will leave me alone." She agreed, because she knew it only takes one touch of His Spirit to forever change your life. I didn't know anything about church, but I felt maybe I should wear a dress, but I didn't have one, so, I told my sister-in-law about my dilemma, and she let me borrow a mini skirt. I remember sitting in a chair next to my mother, with my little mini skirt on, my legs crossed and chewing gum. I was impatient for the service to be over so I could get on with my life.

The pastor's daughter, Wanda Holloway, would bring her keyboard and play and sing before her daddy would preach. But that night she was not able to come, so there was no music. The preacher went straight into his sermon. He was just teaching – he did not get emotional. I don't remember what he was talking about, but then he began to tell a story. It was about the man at the gate called Beautiful.

I had never gone to Sunday school as a child so, I had never heard a bible story before. I was in complete amazement. When the preacher got to the part of the story where Peter took the lame man by the hand, he then took my uncle Odell by the hand and lifted him to his feet to illustrate. Then he said, "and immediately his feet and ankle bones received strength." When he did this, it felt like an arrow went straight into my heart. I fell in love with this Christ he was telling us about. I instantly stood up and raised both hands, tears rolling down my face. I knew I had met the One Aunt Cindy had told me about months before. The second bidder at the auction block I knew was Jesus because I saw and felt his love and compassion.

It was an hour later when I came to myself. Standing in the middle of Aunt Helen's living room, people all around me were praying and crying. I wasn't sure what had happened, but I knew I was changed. Old things had passed away and everything was new. I went to that prayer meeting one person and when I left, I was completely changed. They sing an old song, (I'm in a new world since the Lord saved me.) Well, that was exactly how I felt. I no longer talked the same; I didn't think the same. The things I used to love to do no longer mattered to me. I didn't want to be around my old friends. It was such a change, other than going to church, I just stayed home, trying to sort out what had happened to me.

Well, this was just a Thursday night prayer meeting, but a wind of the Spirit had blown in from nowhere catching everyone by surprise – what it must have been like in the upper room. The pastor asked Aunt Helen if he could come back Friday night just to see what the Lord might do. Sure enough, the power fell, and people prayed for hours. The preacher decided this was a revival and it needed to be moved to a church nearby. Uncle David pastored a church about ten miles down the road. So, Uncle David started a revival that Saturday night at his church. I have to say this was the most inspiring time of my life. This revival continued for six solid weeks. We never took a night off. Every day I couldn't wait to get to church. God was surely on the move, and I wanted to move with Him. During this revival many young people came to the Lord and the church was packed out every night.

5 | THE GAUTREAUX FAMILY

"Barry," Dad said, "come with me to peddle some vegetables. We need to make a few sales today." It was the cold winter's end of 1980. Looking out the window of dad's small farm truck, flint-grey skies looked bleak above the lifeless foliage, a thin layer of frost crystallizing everything it touched. What little heat was in the truck wasn't much, making me wish even more I wasn't here. It seemed dad was going to stop at every house in the neighborhood and try to sell a potato or two. I was pretty sure I could find better use of my time, but dad insisted that I was to come along with him. It had been a very long cold afternoon. As dad and I were just nearing the end of our route for the day, Dad said it was important that we sell our extra vegetables to make ends meet. I knew he was right; I just didn't know why I had to come along.

Thunk! My head hit the window as the truck jolted from a muddy hole and then came to a stop. Honk! Honk! After a few minutes I said, "Dad I don't think anyone is coming out." Anxious to get home and enjoy a hot meal or really anything else besides sitting in this cold truck, Dad said "Wait. I have a friend who lives here." About that time the front door swung open, and a man emerged from inside the house.

"David!" Dad exclaimed. "How are you?"

"As long as I keep pushing wood in that old heater, I'll be fine." he said with a chuckle as he leaned over to look in the back of the truck.

"Looks like you've got a load back here."

As he began to make his order, Dad called out to me, "Barry! Come help us."

Groaning silently inside, I got out of the cab and walked around to the back of the truck. Turning down the tarp and filling a bag with potatoes, a few turnips, and then an onion or two, David walked over and extended his hand, so I shook it.

"It's good to see you, Barry."

I just nodded and kept working. He then walked back over to Dad and said "So, how is Molly?"

"She's got her hands full with all those youngin's, but me and that girl is making it just fine."

David then said "Joe, we are having a revival at the church, and I sure would like for you to come and bring your family." I then looked up to see what my dad would say, but he just gave a polite nod and said, "Well, we better get out of this cold." I went around and got in the truck as they said their goodbyes. Then we drove away. I wondered to myself what Dad thought about the invite to church. We went to one a few times before, but Dad always complained that the preacher was always late and that he smelled bad.

HEADED TO CHURCH

"Ouch! Mom, Barry pinched me!" Tina Gautreaux tattled.

"Barry, you're 17! Please don't be aggravating your sister."

"I wouldn't have to if she wouldn't be kicking my leg!" argued Barry.

Tina whined back, "Mom, I'm not kickin' his leg, I'm swinging mine and his leg is getting in the way.

Joseph had heard enough. "Both of you quit arguing and sit still. There are ten of us in this old two-door Ford car and there is no room for roughhousing. And you kids had better behave tonight. We were invited to this meeting and if . . ."

"SHHHHHH!" his wife interrupted. "Listen. What's that? 'I am on the battlefield for my Lord!' Yes, 'I'm on the battlefield for my Lord!'"

"It's singing!" exclaimed Cathy Gautreaux.

"They sound excited, Mom!" another Gautreaux child said. And for the first time that night as Barry and his family stepped into the little church, they each felt something beyond excitement and curiosity. It was the gentle Spirit of the Holy Ghost drawing them into a hunger for something more than the world could offer. And by the end of that revival meeting, every member of the Gautreaux family, in some way, left changed.

****

It amazes me, how God orchestrates our life, and we just fall into His plan, unaware of it, not knowing that God planned for Barry to be there that night with his family, and that God had hand picked him for this service. There was a crossroads that night, and only Barry could choose which road he was going to take.

****

"The Lord has been so good to me, I feel like traveling on, oh yes I feel like traveling on, until that blessed home, I see I feel like traveling on."

As Barry stood there listening to the singing inside the small country church. People all around him were standing on their feet and clapping enthusiastically – some within rhythm and others not so much, but that didn't seem to hinder anything. He rubbed his hands together unsure of what to do. A man an aisle over started jumping up and down. Barry stared at him, knowing that whatever would make someone want to jump like that, had to be more powerful than him caring what others thought about him. He then looked back towards the couple on the stage where Evangelist Daniel Swinnea and his wife, Betty, were leading the song. The man had his eyes squeezed shut while singing the words, "nor pain or death can enter there…I feel like traveling on." He began to pace back and forth as if he was on a journey in his mind that no one else could see. The man stopped singing and walked back to his wife singing with him beside the piano, with the music still playing never missing a beat, the man then wrapped his arm around his wife as he began to testify.

"Most of you know my wife gave birth to a set of triplets prematurely and even though all three of those little boys fought as hard as they could, they did not make it. But we know they are awaiting us in heaven. And because of that we can sing, I feel like traveling on, because God is with us, and he is moving right now wanting to fill someone with the Holy Ghost and fire!"

The congregation erupted with shouting and praise. Sister Betty now had her hands raised with tears streaming down her face. It was then Barry felt a strong desire to want what Daniel and Betty had. They had something that could allow them to keep wanting to go on strong for the Lord, with such zeal despite such heartbreaking loss. Barry had heard about the Holy Ghost, and he knew in his mind and felt in his heart that he had to have it.

Phillip Holloway placed his guitar on its stand and reached for his Bible and notebook. The time for preaching had come and this young minister knew God had a plan for this service. At 21 years old, Brother Phillip had already made a choice early in life to live a consecrated life before the Lord. The time he spent in prayer for tonight's service had given him the knowledge to know that God wanted to call someone into the ministry. He stood in front of the pulpit and read his text, then bowed his head asking God to anoint him to reach that one that God was calling that night. He raised his head, opened his eyes, looking into the congregation he titled his message "And God called Samuel."

As Barry sat there on the pew, he began to feel conviction and started to look back and forth for a way he could get out of the pew without interrupting the service. Rebellious was the word used to describe his personality. The principal at Barry's high school would say "Barry is soon to graduate but that Gautreaux boy is going to end up in the penitentiary before he is twenty."

I'm sure that his predictions about Barry were correct, but that night God had another plan. The longer he sat there, the more his heart began to pound in his chest. The preacher was preaching with conviction and a fire that drove every word straight into Barry's heart.

After Phillip finished preaching, Barry had indeed heard the call. He went to the altar and gave his life to the Lord. He was changed! He had been touched by the fire of God, so inspired, and walking a new road, nothing was ever the same for him after that night.

Brother Barry would come to church week after week seeking the Holy Ghost. A few months went by, and he had not received it, so he went on a fast. After 17 days of no food and spending as much time as he could, praying and reading his bible, he finally received the Holy Ghost. But he was still so hungry for God and feeling the call to preach, he continued the fast 23 more days, making it a 40-day fast. You might say that sounds impossible. Well, today it is rarely heard of, but back in the day, it was common. We would be so hungry for God, and so full of zeal to work for Him, that we were willing to make sacrifices. Brother Barry became a very successful minister and has continued for more than 40 years. He married a beautiful lady in 1988 – Sister Theresa Rushing from Mississippi, and they have two children who are in the ministry.

Brother Barry's high school principal has given the testimony many times of how God found a young man, no doubt headed for the penitentiary, and turned his life around and called him to preach. The principal recently passed away, and Brother Barry was asked to speak at his funeral because he had made such an impact on his life.

Brother Barry, his siblings and his mom and dad have been like family for 40 years. When God puts someone in your life, it is meant to last forever. Brother Barry said, looking back, one thing he greatly appreciates is how Brother Phillip and his mom and dad took the time to help him, teach and admonish him. There were many times they would invite him into their home, giving him good Christian fellowship, and teaching him the ways of God.

It is so important to take time with new Christians, even more so when they are young.

6 | MY PRINCE

Young and insecure, I was just a girl, with nothing to offer but a broken life that had just been redeemed. We were from two different worlds. I knew nothing about his way of life. He had never been in the world that I had just been redeemed from, a world full of failure and sin. Wearing clothes torn from the rough and cruel world that I had been in. My hair a tangled mess from the road of sin that I had trodden on. Barefoot and beat down from the load I had to bear. My face reflecting the fear that I had lived in and my eyes weak from the lack of nourishment.

This man, this minister was a child of a King. He had everything; a life filled with God. He is so well dressed in his armor: his helmet of salvation, breastplate of righteousness, and his feet covered with the Gospel of peace. He even had a sword and a shield! Such potential to work for the Lord. He has talents and abilities that most people would covet. He had people who loved and supported him. How could someone this wonderful even look my way.

As I see him from day to day, laboring for his heavenly Father, I am sure he hasn't even noticed me. I feel as though, he will never look far enough down to see me. And besides, it's true, I am no longer on that road of grief, but I haven't been completely transformed into the image I am desiring to be. Still ashamed of my past, I am thankful he hasn't noticed me.

But then one day as I am standing in the same place, that I had stood so many times before, thinking that I am invisible to this handsome prince, he then walks over and looked at me with love and compassion in his eyes, and introduces himself. "I am Phillip, and I am a child of a King." He then continues, "My Father sent me to you." How my heart swelled up inside. Not just because this handsome young prince has befriended me, but the fact his Father, the King sent him to me.

This handsome prince commenced to bring me new clothes to wear, and shoes for my feet. Now, I can raise my head, and face the world. He has given me fruits of the spirit to nourish me, and gifts of chocolate to make me smile. My face is beaming as I behold his strength. My eyes now sparkle because of the beauty around me. He then reassures me as we travel together that he will not leave me, and that he will teach me how to be a child of the King.

As we fellowship from day to day, I realize he is a dream come true. How wonderful it would be to embark upon a life's journey with him. Forever be with this strong and ambitious man. He has given me strength when I was weak, and a purpose when I felt there was no hope. He has always reassured me, that I can be what I was created to be. When no one else could see potential in me, he took a chance and proved them wrong.

Then one day, this tall dark handsome prince, dressed in a suit fit for a king, slowly walked up to me. With his head towards the ground, I could tell something was weighing heavy on his mind. As he approaches me, he lifts his head, his face never making an expression of joy or grief. I am speechless! What has happened? He then looks at me with those hazel green eyes, the look that has always made my heart skip a beat. He then reached out and took me by both hands. Then gave a smile that drove away every thought of doubt. He then began to express his feelings that have developed towards me over the past months. He confessed... "In the beginning, I came to you because my Father sent me. And although you were still a little tattered from the life you once lived, you, were very beautiful. As we have spent time together, I realize you are a diamond, and to me a priceless treasure. I feel complete when I am with you, and I don't think I can be all that I am intended to be, without you. In the short time that you have been redeemed, you have become more than anyone expected you to be. To me, you have become the woman I have fallen in love with. So, you see, my Father didn't send me on a mission of mercy on your part, but on mine. He knew I needed you."

As he is reaching into his pocket, he is also bending on one knee. I am speechless, my heart is pounding out of my chest, surely this is the moment that will change my life forever. I heard him say, in a sweet calm voice,

"Bonetta, Will you marry me?"

This moment will forever be etched in my mind, how could a handsome prince be in love with, 'Just a Girl,' I could hardly speak. But in a shattered tear-filled voice, I then said, "Yes."

Now this wonderful man is teaching me, to see myself through the eyes of the heavenly Father. The image of a girl dressed in worldly rags, bare foot and unprotected from the destruction of sin, has been dimmed, by the vision of a young lady with a garment of modesty and shoes to walk upon the pitfalls of destruction, she will be united with a man of God. He will help guide her in the light and truth of Jesus Christ. Finally, the moment I had so waited for, and what seemed would only be a fairytale, has now become reality, when a common, 'little girl,' finally, gets her prince. And now here I stand, with my head held high, in my white laced dress that flows so elegantly all the way to the floor. With every hair in place; capped by a beautiful sheer veil, slightly exposing the calm disposition of my face, and the curiosity in my eyes. And for my feet, shoes embellished with tiny little pearls, to carry me so delicately. Full of excitement, I tightly clinched a beautiful bouquet of flowers. As I make my way towards my handsome prince, for the first time in my life, I feel like a princess. I am ready to embark upon this journey with God, and my prince.

'THE LOVE STORY'

The sound of saints had filled the sanctuary; their praise was ringing through the hills and hollows of the little country village. Such a presence of the Lord in that little wood frame church, as the whole congregation was singing in one accord. I can remember so vividly as the words rang out, when the redeemed are gathering in, washed like snow and free from sin. How we'll shout and how we'll sing when the redeemed are gathered in."

Phillip has preached another sermon at this six-week revival, that has changed the lives of so many people. As it is nearing the end of the service, he takes a seat on the front pew. He then wipes the sweat off his brow as the Spirit directs his attention towards a girl; she is standing with her hands lifted and weeping in the presence of God. Just then his heart skips a beat, and the Spirit then says to him, "This girl I have redeemed from a life of sin, she is to be your wife."

THE VALENTINE

Just A Girl, A Journey With God

It was a cold, but beautiful winter evening. The stars twinkled like little diamonds in the sky. I felt a sudden chill to the bone as the crisp wind softly blew into my face.

Finally, I found our car in the dark parking lot of that little country church. Sliding into the passenger seat, to patiently wait for mom to finish her goodbyes, I noticed a box of valentine candy laying there.

Just to see the little heart shaped box with a bow on top and knowing that it is filled with delicious chocolates, can send any girl's heart into a flutter. But this wonderful little box of candy holds a mystery. There is no name on it, so, to whom does it belong?

Do I have a secret admirer?

Or did someone just accidently put it into the wrong car?

As I began to ponder these thoughts, I heard mothers' footsteps as she approached the car. Her face lit up with excitement when she saw that little heart shaped box. "What have you got there?" she exclaimed! I then held up the box of chocolates. And in a confused tone I answered, "Well, it's a valentine for someone, but there is no name on it so, it's not mine."

The following afternoon when we arrived for church, I was a bit surprised. As the car rolled to a stop, Phillip opened my door and immediately began to inquire about a box of chocolates. He said, "Did you by any chance find a box of chocolates in your car last night?"

Feeling an instant relief that I have found the rightful owner of this mystery candy. I immediately said, "Yes, I did!" and quickly turned around and picked up the box to hand it to him.

"No, no it's for you" as he began to talk in a nervous stutter, "I mean, I am the one who left it there for you." I thanked him, and he turned and walked away.

This valentine left me a bit confused. Phillip never said another word to me for the duration of that six-week revival. I had just found a brand-new life and didn't want to set myself up for a big disappointment. So, I decided to rule the gift as a friendly gesture and move on with my life. If it was more than that, he would have personally handed them to me or least would have put my name on it. What I didn't know, at the time, was that Phillip was too bashful to hand the valentine to me personally so, he just put them in my car during the service. After he got home, he realized that he didn't put either of our names on it. This meant he had to intervene, just in case I had someone else in mind, and would think it came from them.

'THE YES'

As I am trying to process all the wonderful things that has happened to me over the past few months. I stepped out onto the church parking lot. Finally, it was spring, we had endured another cold harsh winter. It was also the last Sunday morning of the six-week revival that had changed my life. As I was standing there, the March wind was gently blowing through my hair, and I was just admiring all the new life that had sprang up. The beautiful bright shades of green in the trees, and the wonderful fragrance of honey suckle that filled the air. The life I once lived was so far behind me, and now I am 'embarking upon this journey with God.'

As I turned around, there stands Phillip. He began to talk. I noticed that he is nervous, his face is flushed, and he is searching for words to say. Finally, he asked me to have lunch with him the next day. I was awe stricken that someone so anointed and talented would ask me out on a date. And somehow, at the same time, so honored.

The "yes," I gave him that day would begin a life's long journey between a twenty-old year old, successful handsome minister, and a little forteen year old girl who had nothing to offer but a broken life that had just been redeemed.

The word successful brings a twist to the story. Phillip was still young, and his ministry was doing so well, everyone (the elders of the church), agreed that he needed a wife. Someone to share the work of the ministry. But they all had their own ideas to what her criteria needed to be. Definitely someone mature, and gifted, preferably musically inclined and a singer. So, with all of that in mind, it wasn't anything personal, but I wasn't the best candidate. Must I say it was no small stir when Phillip began a courtship with a little fourteen year old girl, who had only been in church for a few months.

'ANOTHER YES'

It was hardly a month into our courtship when I heard a knock on the door. What a delightful surprise when I opened the door, and there stood Phillip. I could tell something was on his mind, I invited him in, and enquired to what was the reason for the visit.

He said, "I need to discuss something with you,"

Just then, thoughts of fear that he was going to break up with me flooded my mind. Afterall, why else would he just show up so unexpectedly? As we sat there on the sofa, he began to express his feelings towards me. He began to remind me of how young I was. I was certain by this time that he had decided to put all of this behind him and move on with his life, but then he reminded me,

"You know the Lord told me that you would be my wife."
"Yes," I replied.

He continued, "Well, I realize you are very young, and I don't want you to feel pressured in any way, but as soon as you feel you are ready, I am ready to marry you."

Just then my heart skipped a beat. I had just set myself up for the worst and he gives me a gentle proposal. For a brief moment, I didn't know what to say. Finally, I replied, "More than anything, I want to marry you. Although I am very young, I trust you. I trust that you will provide for me, but more than that, you will protect me, teach me, and as we walk together, I am confident you will be patient until I become the wife I am ordained to be. So, the answer is 'yes,' I am ready to be your wife."

Soon the word was out, and when some of the church heard the news that Phillip had intensions to marry me, it soon became what seemed like a war zone. Everyone expressing their thoughts and opinions. Each one sharing all the reasons why this marriage will never work. I was pretty sure that Phillip would think I wasn't worth the fight, but on the contrary, he had heard from God and was determined to make this work.

Some instructed him to be careful. Others just simply opposed the idea. It was like a huge whirlwind over our heads. Everyone in the church was trying to detour what they thought was a disaster in the making.

Phillip determined to avoid the turmoil, suggested we get married right away. So, we set a date for May 30th, 1980. Which was only six weeks away. Phillip's mom and dad were supportive of our decision, and so were my parents. So, it was settled.

My mother went right to work, making plans to have a big, beautiful wedding. She ordered the cake right away; it was to be a three tier. Then, no time to waste the bridal shower, which by the way was a huge success; I couldn't imagine needing all that stuff. All the flowers, my dress, the invitations and so many small details. My mother was very hyper and loved to do things like weddings and parties. So, she was like a runaway train. But just three days before the wedding, it all ended in a screeching halt. So, now the church takes a sigh of relief, and the tables are turned in my direction.

Brother Daniel Swinnea, a man of God who was well respected and completely in favor of the wedding, was awaken by a dream. He dreamed that Phillip and I were standing before the preacher at our wedding and he saw the word "Ichabod" written over our heads. Which means, "the glory of the Lord has departed." After he had awakened, he knew he had to warn us. When he revealed his dream to us, we were devastated, and I must admit, I was confused. God had spoken to Phillip that I would be his wife and now we are being told if we do get married, the glory of the Lord will depart.

Phillip and I decided to get alone and make our decision, without anyone else giving their opinion. After spending some time in prayer, we then decided that the best thing to do was to postpone the wedding for a few months and work through this whole thing.

The first order of business was to tell our parents. His parents agreed that it was the right thing to do, but my mom did not take it so well. She had put so much time and money into this wedding. There were just three days until my wedding day, and we have changed our minds. She was furious. Not so much because we postponed the wedding, but she really thought Phillip had gotten cold feet, or that someone had changed his mind about me. She did not understand that maybe the timing was not right. Or, that God was just trying us, to see if we would be obedient to him, no matter how difficult it would be.

We didn't intend to cancel the wedding altogether, just postpone it for a little while, and set another date for the near future. Mom began to call everyone and cancel all the plans, telling everyone that Phillip had stood me up and wasn't going to marry me. Mom was hurt and offended. Looking from her perspective, I completely understood how she was feeling. But nonetheless, I had to stand for what I felt was right in my heart. Mom continued day after day to tell me that Phillip didn't love me and that he would never marry me. She would often say, "He is just making a fool out of you." And for a little insecure fourteen year old girl, it was hard not to believe her words. She was angry and bitter about the whole thing and wanted me to feel the same way. But what she didn't realize, I had no desire to be angry or bitter. And no intensions to backslide on God. Even if it didn't work out between Phillip and me, I was in love with Jesus. My heart was set like a flint. I had been smitten by this wonderful presence of God. So, I wasn't continuing going to church hoping things would work out between Phillip and me, I was continuing going to church because I have a life with God. If Phillip is meant to be a part of it, then God will make it happen, and if not, I will continue to serve God anyway.

Finally, mom decided that I could no longer see Phillip. She would not allow him to come over, and I could not go anywhere with him. We attended the same church, so that was the only time we could see each other. After a few months mom determined to distant us completely. She even threatened to stop my church attendance. Dad stepped up and assured me that would never happen. He was a quiet man and picked his battles. I have learned over the years, just because you see clearly what God is doing in your life, it doesn't mean everyone else does. So, when people are trying to discourage you, are maybe you feel that they are unfairly fighting you, be patient with them. They don't have the understanding you do. You obey God, no matter who it offends, and God will take care of everything else.

MARRIED AT LAST

It was now October and our church had been in revival with Brother Smith, an elder from Arkansas. He had been there all week, but it was Sunday evening and the revival had ended. Tomorrow Brother Smith would be heading home. Sometime during the night, the Lord gave him one more message to deliver. The next morning right at daybreak Phillip heard a horn blowing outside. He went out to see who it was. There sat Brother Smith in his old 1970 Ford Torino. That old Torino was setting there idling and the whole car was shaking and making a loud noise.

The windshield had straps across it to keep it secure, but he was not at all ashamed.

As Phillip approached the car, Brother Smith said, "Son, I don't know what you are praying about, but God said, go ahead and do what you feel is right in your heart." He then rolled up his window and drove away.

Phillip didn't waste any time to tell me the wonderful news. He knew he wasn't allowed at my house and not wanting to face the wrath of my mother, he decided to give me a call. Phones were much different in 1980. There were no cell phones and the one phone the whole family used, was hanging on the wall. Party lines were still popular in those days. A party line could have up to three houses on it. That meant if you picked up the phone and someone was talking on it, you just eased it back down very quietly and waited for your turn. You then tried again and again until it was free. I'm sure some of those old time, gossipers listened in before they put the phone down. By this time we had a private line. We were some of the first ones in our community to get a private line. I remember feeling so proud like we were really moving up in the world.

When he told me what Brother Smith had said, I was so excited! Phillip then said, "I am ready to marry you, but you are fourteen years old. One of your parents will have to sign the marriage license." Well, I knew I couldn't ask mom, and honestly, I wasn't sure that dad would be willing to sign either. I knew it would take a miracle. My dad worked five days a week putting up electrical high lines. Many times, his work would take him away from home. Currently, he was working local. My dad was a hard worker. I never knew him to take a day off, not even if he was sick.

Just A Girl, A Journey With God

On Tuesday, October 7th, 1980, as I walked out onto the porch, there was dad sitting in his rocking chair. Like a man on a mission, before I could even ask him why he wasn't at work.

He said, "Sissy, when you get ready to get married, I'll sign your marriage license for you."

My dad was a sweet Christian man. I had no doubt that God had instructed him to do this. Without hesitation, I replied, "I am ready now."

He then explained, "We need to go today while your mother is working, and don't say a word to anyone for three days because if she finds out, she will have it annulled." Dad was always a peace maker. I knew this could not be easy for him. It was definitely a risky mission because if mom finds out, it would be an all-out war. I called Phillip, and the three of us immediately went to the courthouse in Ville Platte, Louisiana, and dad signed the marriage license. We didn't tell a soul until Friday afternoon, (after the courthouse had closed for the weekend). Mom never said anything to me. I guess dad took the whole blow of things, but to avoid the tension, we decided to move forward very quickly.

The wedding was to be on the following Sunday October 12th, just two days after we made our announcement. Naturally, I didn't get the big wedding we had planned six months before. It was only a few family members and friends that gathered in our little country church. My face beaming with pride as dad walked me down the aisle, and at that moment, I felt as though I was the luckiest girl in the whole world. Our Pastor, Brother Dillard Holloway preformed the ceremony, "I now pronounce you man and wife" never sounded so sweet.

But now at last! We are united in Holy Matrimony, and ready to embark upon our journey together and make our mark in this wonderful world.

DESPISE NOT THE DAY OF SMALL THINGS

It was a Sunday and the beautiful morning sun had just peaked above the trees. I was finishing my first cup of coffee when Phillip pulled into the driveway in his old Chevrolet van. The day was October 12th, 1980. I didn't see any of my family before I slipped out the door to meet Phillip. This would be the last day; that I would call the little town of Turkey Creek my home. To think of it today more than forty years later, it is a bit emotional, but that day it was nothing but excitement.

We would be attending church that Sunday morning at 10 a.m. but first, we went to the Winn Dixie to purchase the cake that would be served after our wedding, of which would take place at 2 p.m. that afternoon. It wasn't a special-ordered cake. We just walked in and bought what they had available. It was a sheet cake with blue roses on it and it only costed $14.95. That day we were proud to call it our wedding cake, and today more than forty years later I am still proud of it because it reminds me of how innocent we were.

After we left there, I met my dear friend Linda. She would try her best to make her wedding dress fit my small-framed body. The dress was so elegant and beautiful. I can still remember feeling like a princess that day. She then insisted that I also borrowed her shoes because the heels would be high enough to pick me up and keep me from tripping over my dress. I had asked my friend Kathy to be my maid of honor, and Phillip asked my brother Kent to be his best man.

As soon as the Sunday morning service had ended, we began all the preparations to get ready for the not so big wedding. Finally, as my parent's car pulled into the church parking lot, I noticed that dad was alone. Mom was still upset with dad for signing my marriage license for me and didn't come to the wedding.

Not a lot of people attended the wedding but then again, we only had two days to get the word out before the wedding day. Finally, it was 2 o'clock and time to walk the aisle. I will never forget the delightful feeling when first Kathy and Kent walked in that little country church. Dad and I walked in right behind them. There I was in my beautiful dress, feeling like a princess, and making my way towards my handsome prince. Pastor Dillard Holloway preformed the ceremony. Phillip and I made our vows to love and to hold, in sickness and in health, till death do we part. Then we gathered under the old oak tree for the little reception and just then mom drove up. Yes, she was able to move past some of the hurt and come. And even though she was late I was so glad she at least came.

We didn't have a big honeymoon planned, simply because we didn't have the money. But that didn't matter to me because now, I am with my prince. I am confident there will be a happily ever after. At 6 p.m. that afternoon we went to church, and the next morning Phillip got up and went to work. But at last! we are now married and ready to embark on our life's journey.

I had no real knowledge of where that day would lead me. But like a seed that a farmer would so very carefully place into the soil, that he had prepared, in hopes that one day it would sprout into the beautiful flora that it was meant to be, God had placed me with this man of God so that I could flourish into what he intended for me. If only I could have seen from the beginning what God was doing. Instead, at first like the seed that is planted beneath the sod, it seemed all I experienced was darkness and confusion. And I must admit sometimes I had questions to why I am here. In many ways it felt like a death to me because I was so young and now, I was placed somewhere so unfamiliar.

Please don't misunderstand me, my prince was everything I thought he would be and more. He attended my every need and tried to prevent any tears from falling. If one would slipped pass from time to time, he was there to quickly dry it. He would remind me daily how his love for me only grew stronger. But this struggle was coming from within, simply because there was a death taking place in me, from the little girl that I am to the Woman God had ordained me to be.

When a farmer is holding that tiny little seed in his hand, he can hardly imagine that it can become something beautiful and fruitful. And while it is still under the sod, he is not sure that it has the life in it that he has hoped for. That little seed will first gain a few roots then germination begins, and the seed sprouts and slowly emerges from the top of the soil and that is when the farmer has faith that it will produce. In the early years of our marriage, I felt much like that little seed. I often wondered if I had the ability in me to be all that God had set before me. It seemed every day I was pushing against the clod that was lying so heavily upon me. Now I realize the key was to push. As I just kept pushing against the daily changes, soon I saw a little sprout. At first the sprout isn't appealing to anyone, but at least we know the seed has life.

Never despise the day of small things they are the beginning of something wonderful.

So now, here I am, a fifteen-year-old girl a young Christian and a new wife. It was definitely new territory for me. I was eager to learn and willing to be the person that God had ordained for me to be, but I had no idea how hard it would be to become that new creation. Not only was I a young new wife but I am a preacher's wife. I felt the pressure and expectations of everyone just waiting to see if I could be transformed into the successful roll of a wife, and even more a preacher's wife. Would I be that seed that rotted under the sod and never produced anything, or would I be successful?

Because I was insecure and had low self-esteem, I had begun to think I had made a big mistake. I was constantly telling myself that I was not capable of being a wife much less a preacher's wife. Part of my insecurity stemmed from the fact I was so young and part because I had quit school when I was thirteen and had little education. I didn't share my feelings of insecurity with anyone because I was afraid it would show weakness and people would doubt me. As I would battle with it from time-to-time, Phillip would come home from work and find me crying. He thought I was homesick and even though I assured him that was not the issue he persisted to comfort me and try to persuade me to be patient that this would pass. It was during these times that I discerned how much he truly loved me and believed in me. Looking back, I am sure that Phillip didn't realize how insecure I was and how much I battle with low-self-esteem, but God used him to bring me out of it. Shortly after we were married, he began on a daily basis to tell me how beautiful I was and that he believed in me. I needed to hear that, and God knew it.

The bible says that the power of life and death is in the power of the tongue. I can say I have experienced that scripture in my life firsthand. Phillips words from day to day began to build me up and I could feel the sincere confidence that he had in me. Finally, it had begun to take root. It was just a root but like the seed under the clod I am sure that it is going to sprout.

The first year of any marriage, is the hardest and ours was no exception. I have always felt like our relationship was like a fairytale, but even fairytales have difficulties. During that first year Phillip and I got along just fine. But I had a hard time getting past what I thought people expected me to be. I realize now it was just a mind battle that I should have overcome but I didn't know how at the time.

Mom was still not going to church during this time. I would ask her on a continual basis to come with me, but she never would. We had been married about eight months when our home church had begun revival with an Evangelist from Monroe, Louisiana. I had invited mom to come, but I did not expect her to this time. In the past, she always turned me down. It was now the middle of the week and I had become very discouraged with my progress of being a successful preacher's wife. I had convinced myself that Phillip would be better off without me. Phillip had left for church an hour early and was going to come back and pick me up. While he was gone, I packed my suitcase. As I was headed for the door to go to my neighbor's house (I was going to borrow their phone to call my mom to come and get me.) Just as I put my hand on the doorknob, someone knocked on the door. When I opened it, there stood my mother. I stood there for a second in shock then I asked her to come inside. As she was walking in the door she said, "I came to go to church with you tonight if that is ok." I knew I had to make a decision right then and there would I go forward with my marriage and trust God to keep me or tell mom that I quit. Well, it only took a moment to decide because I knew God had planned the whole thing and that He knew I would make the right decision. God was showing me that even my mother had confidence in Phillip and me. I knew if mom had faith in me then I needed to have faith in myself.

I never told mom that I had my suitcase packed to leave that day. Mom didn't get saved until many years later, but God used her that night.

MARRIAGE

Finding a spouse is a major part of your life, because this person will affect your life in every way. He or she will determine how you will serve God, and how you will raise your family. It will also determine rather you are happy are not. So, it is important to fast a pray and never rush into a decision that will determine your life's destiny.

Phillip and I have been married for more than forty years. We have kept our love for God and each other, fresh and fervent. We have always tried to put ministry and our walk with God first in our lives. We have not always been perfect, but our intensions have been right. I think one thing that has kept us on track was the dream that God gave Brother Daniel before we were married. When he saw, "Ichabod" over our heads. It made us realize that if we don't give our all, the enemy will send something our way to steal the glory of God from our lives.

7| IN SEARCH OF FAITH

Robert's healing

I was such a young Christian and had so much to learn. Phillip grew up in a family that fully trusted God. His Parents became Christians during the early 50's. A.A. Allen, Jack Coe, Oral Roberts, and many other healing preachers were popular then. So, it was only natural that in those days people believed in miracles. Phillip's mother, Mildred Elaine Holloway, was the first one to get saved in their community. His dad, Willard Holloway, was in the army and stationed in Germany, at the time.

It all began when Brother John Temple a minister from Rayville, Louisiana and his wife Clara were praying one night before they went to bed. Sister Clara began to give out tongues of interpretation and started spelling a word. Brother Temple then wrote down the letters she had spelled out, (L E C O M P T E) He had no idea what it meant. God then spoke to him and said, "Go south and look for Robert Brown."

Brother Temple found the small town of Lecompte on the map, and it was just two hours away. So, the following weekend he went to Lecompte, and sure enough he found Robert Brown. Brother Temple shared with Mr. Brown what had happened in prayer, and that he wanted to come on the weekends and hold prayer meetings in his home. He didn't know anything about God, but he said, "If that is what God said then he was willing to do it."

Just A Girl, A Journey With God

Robert Brown lived across the street from Mary Brady who was Willard's sister. With Willard being in Germany, Mildred would often stay with Mary.

Mildred and Willard had one child at this time, Robert Lee. He was eighteen months old. Robert had asthma, and in those days, they didn't offer Medicaid. Not having insurance they were forced to rely on old home remedies. One Saturday morning in September of 1954, Mildred was sitting on Mary's front porch. She was trying to relax and give Robert a gentle bounce on her knee to console him. The cold he had taken, along with the asthma he suffered from, made it difficult for him to breathe. Just then a man walked up to the porch. "Hello ma'am," he said, in a low tone. "I am John Temple from Rayville, and I am staying with Mr. Brown for the weekend. We are going to have a prayer meeting tonight at his house. We would love to have you, if you would like to come."

She then replied, with a simple "thank you." As Brother Temple was talking to her, he noticed that Robert was struggling to breathe. He then asked, "What is wrong with your baby?" "He has asthma and has taken a cold," she replied. He said, "Do you mind if I pray for him, I believe God can heal him." She didn't know this man and had never heard that God could heal. She was a little skeptic but, willing to do anything for her baby. She then said to him in a doubtful tone, "I guess it wouldn't hurt anything." Brother Temple then walked over and put both hands on Robert's head. Mildred never taking her eyes off of Robert for a second. Brother Temple then prayed a simple prayer. "Lord heal this baby for your glory, Amen." Mildred said, Robert's breathing instantly became normal. She was astounded, but so grateful. Then without a second thought, she looked at Brother Temple and said, "I will be at that prayer meeting tonight."

She went that night and gave her heart to God. She immediately began to seek for the Holy Ghost. She wrote her husband in Germany and said, "I have given my life to God, and I want to pay tithes." He wrote her back and told her, "Do whatever you feel is right, and when I get home, I will attend church with you." And that is exactly what he did. God used Mildred and Willard in many ways over the years. They had many hardships, but God was indeed faithful to them.

I am the God that healeth

Mildred and her family saw many miracles. They trusted God, not only for healing, but anything they might need. Mildred was such a prayer warrior and inspired me to be just like her.

Phillip and I had only been married a year or so when I began to have trouble with my kidneys. I didn't want to see a doctor, I wanted to trust God for my healing, just like Phillip and his family did. So, I wasn't sure what was wrong, but I was having chills and fever. I felt like I needed to urinate but couldn't. It would get better then start all over again. I prayed and asked God to heal me but I didn't seem to be getting anywhere. I began to think that healing was only for a certain kind of people, and I was not one of them.

One night, around midnight, Phillip was fast asleep, I was setting up in the bed with my knees propped up, my bible laying across my lap, I said to God, "I want to trust you to heal me, just like Phillip's family does, but I'm not sure how." I then expressed to God, "I need to know if you are going to be my Healer or not. If you are not, I am going to the doctor's for help." It may seem bold, but I needed an answer. With my bible in my lap, I then prayed, "Lord I am going to close my eyes, open my bible, and put my finger on a scripture. Whatever it says, I will take as my answer." So, I did. I closed my eyes opened the bible. I put my finger on the page. When I opened my eyes, my finger was on Exodus 15:26: "If thou wilt diligently hearken to the voice of the Lord thy God, and wilt do that which is right in his sight, and wilt give ear to his commandments, and keep all his statutes, I will put none of these diseases upon thee, which I have brought upon the Egyptians: for I am the Lord that healeth thee." My faith grew at that very moment; this was so real! I knew this was a personal message to me from God. I was so excited to know that I too, could trust God. I felt like that night He included me. I didn't realize when you are a child of God, you are already included in everything God has.

I have often tried the same technique, (closing my eyes putting my finger on a scripture), but it would always say something like "flee to the mountains" or "Jesus wept." It never relates to what I am praying about. God is an awesome God. He seldom works the same way twice. We must stay attentive to His voice and follow hard after Him. He did not heal me that night, but now I can pray in faith, knowing He does hear me and will answer my prayers. As I began to seek God for my healing, I would get better, then a few months later, I would start hurting again. I didn't realize it, but my kidneys had been affected by the fact that I grew up drinking Coca Cola. I never drank water or really anything but Coca Cola. It was what my parents drank so that is what they bought for us. My mother lived to be seventy-eight, and my dad turned ninety three days before he passed. They both drank Coca Cola until the day they died. We have been uniquely formed by

Bonetta Holloway

God, so, just because something is ok for someone else it may not be for you.

One day in prayer, the Lord spoke to me. He didn't speak out loud but in my heart. He said, "If you will stop drinking Coca Cola, I will heal you." My first thought was, I can't stop drinking them. It was at that moment I realized, I am addicted. I just kept praying thinking somehow God will understand my weakness and heal me anyway. But He did not! We were holding a revival at Old Davis town church in Anniston, Alabama. It was a Sunday afternoon and I had been in pain and running fever for a few days. Finally, I couldn't take it anymore. I made up my mind that whatever it takes, I need healing. So, I surrendered and made the commitment to quit them, I said to God " Lord I will stop drinking Coca Cola if you will heal me."

I really thought it would be a challenge for me to quit them. I was so addicted, I would often walk a mile to the store just to get a Coca Cola. I even found pleasure when I would catch the aroma of one. But that day, when I finally committed myself and gave them up, the pain stopped instantly. The fever left and the desire to drink Coca Cola left with it. That was more than thirty-eight years ago. Since that day, I have never desired to drink another one. I have given birth to six children, and I have never had a problem with my kidneys. I have not even had an UT infection. My husband and children drink them occasionally, but it has never been a temptation to me. Sometimes trusting God means you will have to give up things you like. God does not require things of us to be mean. But He does know what is best for us. He also said the willing and obedient would eat the good of the land. I never missed Coca Cola. God already knew He was going to deliver me from the desire of them, but He wanted me to trust Him.

8 | ON THE BAYOU

The beautiful Southern landscape, near Jeanerette, Louisiana, holds a special place in my heart, with its winding bayous and swamp lands, giving the feel of an exotic paradise. Those bayous are filled with unique wildlife such as pelicans and alligators. It is a rare beauty that can only be seen in the deep south. The wonderful people, who live there with their Cajun dialect and unique culture, makes them the most amazing people on earth. These amazing people have created some of the best recipes in the world and bringing a state of bliss to the southern cuisine. When it comes to seafood gumbo, Etouffee, and Jambalaya no one does it like the Cajun kitchens in south Louisiana.

Jessie and Annie Higgins raised their children in a little settlement near Jeanerette. They gave it the name Higgins Hill. The fish market that Jesse owned there, supplied the Higgins family with the means to thrive on the southern bayou. Their house was set right on the bank of Bayou Teche. That muddy bayou provided the experience they needed to become master fisherman.

The Higgins family not only were successful in freshwater fishing, but shrimping was a big part of their lives as well. Shrimp season was from mid-August to mid-December. During this time, it was important to spend as much time as possible in the gulf.

In August of 1982, Phillip and I held a revival there on

Higgins Hill. The next week, Lee and Mitzi Higgins, invited us to join them on their first shrimp run for the season. We were all just young kids at the time. They were in their early twenties, but I was only seventeen. We were very excited to have the opportunity to join them in this adventure. I must say, it was the experience of a lifetime. We boarded the small wooden shrimp boat, (Purple Heart), and made our way through the bayou. The warm sun beaming down on me, and the gentle breeze blowing into my face, brought such peace and tranquility, and reminded me of my creator. As we made our way through the tall cypress trees, with moss hanging from there branches, I noticed there were birds of all kinds finding refuge in them. In the midst of the little cypress knee's, growing up through the water, were the eyes of an alligator bobbing just above the surface. He was snugged just near the bank. It was a unique display of God and His creation. Soon we reached the open waters. With nothing but blue skies, salt water, and a few dolphins trying to keep up with the boat, there was a peaceful excitement to this amazing adventure. Shortly, we were in the gulf, miles from land, and we would be here for seven days. The first few days were heaven on earth. There were no phones, and no hustle and bustle of the city. There wasn't even a bird singing. I would set on the deck for hours and listen to the waves beat against the boat, with a peaceful salty breeze blowing in my face. I felt as as though I could live here forever.

But the dawning of the fourth day brought a change to this peaceful scene. When suddenly, a squall came up, and the wind began to blow violently, tossing the boat up and down in the water. The rain was falling so hard, it was impossible to see. The lightning flashing against the sky and then straight down towards the boat. I wasn't prepared for such a demonstration of the weather. The little cabin, on the boat wasn't enough comfort to make me feel safe during this violent storm. When the storm had passed the sun came out, and the beautiful blue sky brought a peace like I had never experienced. It was as though nothing had happened. In the open waters a storm doesn't leave behind damage to the landscape. You don't see mud holes. So, when the storm passes, it is as if, it had never happened. We didn't realize it at the time, but lightning had struck the boat. The batteries were not working to crank the engine, so we just drifted for hours. I began to have flash backs of the childhood movie, "Gilligan's Island," and I was about to panic. Thankfully, I saw a shrimp boat with the name Sue Ellan written on the side of it. It was Jesse and Annie Higgins. We had no idea they were out there, but I sure was glad to see them. I don't think they were even shrimping. Looking back, I realize they were just good parents out there, watching over their children.

All of this was just another day on the job for them. Thankfully they were able to fix the problem with no issues and the next morning, we were shrimping again. The next day as Mitzi and I were preparing lunch, we noticed that the stoves propane tank was leaking. So, the guys decided to toss it overboard, not realizing the salt water would turn the leaking propane tank into a torpedo. It was violently shooting up and down in the water, coming towards the boat, then away again. Finally, it all stopped when the propane tank was empty, and the tank then safely sank into the water. A few nights later, sometime after midnight, Phillip and I awoke at the same time. We had a strange feeling that our feet were higher than our head. We realized the boat was sinking. Phillip immediately woke Lee up. Because the boat was made of wood, water would continually seep in it. When the water would get to a certain level, a pump would come on and pump out the excess water. Somehow, a piece of trash was caught in the pump, causing it to malfunction. The boat was taking on too much water, causing it to sink. The pump was located under a compartment that held a ton of ice. The ice was being stored to keep the shrimp fresh until we could get back to land. Phillip and Lee had to shovel ice for an hour before they could fix the pump. Finally, the problem was taken care of, and by this time it was time to start to work. Besides all the trouble we had that week, we didn't catch enough shrimp to even take care of the expense of this trip. Lee and Mitzi accused Phillip and I of being a Jonah to them. It was an ongoing joke for many years. We have made wonderful memories with the Higgins family over the years, and we love and respect them very much.

Free as the wind

During the first five years of our marriage, we didn't have any children. We were as free as the wind. Phillip was a roofer by trade, and worked for his family. When he needed to take off it was not a problem. Many times, when he would take off, we would be traveling for revivals. But sometimes we just like to take trips and go sightseeing. I am thankful that God put a space in our marriage before He blessed us with our beautiful family. We always desired to have children and never did anything to prevent it from happening. So, God in His perfect and divine order gave them to us as He saw fit.

We had nieces and nephews that we loved to spend time with. We would take them to the park, or maybe to McDonalds to get a burger. But I remember one time in particular when our little niece, Candace, was two years old, she decided she wanted to come home with us and stay the night. We were young and had no idea what we were getting into. Well, we brought her home with us and she played and laughed. We had a great time until it got dark. She decided quickly that she wanted her mommy. We didn't want to take her back home; we wanted to prove to ourselves and everyone else that we were ready for children of our own. So, we decided to tough it out. We thought that she would soon cry herself to sleep, and all would be well, but she did not. The road in front of our house ran along the bayou, so, shortly after midnight Phillip said, "Let's put her in the car and we will cruise that winding road along the bayou and maybe she will fall asleep." Sure enough it worked. Finally, the crying stopped, and she fell asleep. At two a.m. we returned home and endeavored to put her to bed. Phillip suggested we put her in the bed with us. Maybe it will be comforting to her, and she will stay asleep, so we did. She thankfully did not wake up. What a relief!! We then, so very carefully, got into bed making sure not to wake her. Then at three a.m. I felt something warm and wet draining underneath me. Phillip said to me, "Don't move. I know she wet the bed but if we move her, she will start crying again." But of course, we could not lie there very long. I tried to put something dry underneath her without waking her. That did not work. Sure enough, the crying started up again. Bright and early the next morning we took her home. It was a lesson well learned, and this was the one and only time we kept any of our nieces or nephews overnight.

9 | A BABY OF OUR OWN!!

After almost five years of marriage, I was able to share the wonderful news that we were going to have a baby. We were so excited! We didn't have insurance and Medicaid wasn't available for us at this time. I told Phillip we could use the charity hospital in Pineville, Louisiana. It wasn't as nice as the pay hospitals, but I didn't mind. It was settled, until my mother found out our intentions. "My daughter is not going to that hospital," she exclaims! Phillip decided to do things her way because he didn't want to jeopardize the relationship that he had worked so hard to establish with her. She wanted me to use the Ville Platte Memorial Hospital. The cost for delivery was $1500 and then there were the doctor fees. They required full payment upon arrival. That doesn't sound like much now but in 1985, it was a lot. Phillip was a roofer and back then it didn't pay a lot. The work wasn't always steady. So, we had to save every penny we could to make this happen. Thankfully, by the time I went into labor, we had the money. Phillip was so proud to be able to do this for me and our new baby. To top it off, this would please his mother-in-law. so here we are in this nice hospital feeling good about ourselves.

But after several hours of labor, the doctor came in and said, "I have found some complications with the baby, and I want to do an immediate c-section; without it your baby could die." I was so scared to have this done but not willing to take a chance with the baby, we agreed. Oh, the anxiety I was feeling as a host of nurses came storming into my room prepping me for surgery.

Just A Girl, A Journey With God

No one was allowed to be in there with me. They informed me of how they were going to put me to sleep, open me up, and remove my baby. They would then use staples to put me back together. That was quite a thought for a nineteen year-old girl; I never felt so alone in my life. Phillip was standing in the waiting room looking out the window at the helicopter that was prepared for takeoff. They were going to fly our baby straight to the children's hospital in New Orleans, Louisiana. He was out there alone, praying for God to help me and our baby. We didn't know if we were having a boy, or a girl. It really didn't matter we just wanted our baby to be healthy.

It wasn't long before the surgery was complete. The doctor came through the metal doors where Phillip was waiting. He never looked at Phillip. He just kept walking and said, there is nothing wrong with Elvira. Phillip knew it was an expression the doctor was using to say that it was a girl, and she was loud… and healthy. We were so relieved! On February 6, 1985, we had an eight pound baby girl, Michelle Elaine Holloway and she was perfect. Now, because of the surgery, our hospital bill totaled $5,000.00. The hospital wanted full payment before I could leave. I could only imagine the hopelessness Phillip was feeling at this time. He finally found a bank that would loan him the money. We paid the hospital and took our baby girl home.

Six weeks had passed, and it was time for my final doctor's visit. The doctor informed me that I needed to listen to him closely. He continued with, "You cannot have a baby natural and don't ever let anyone try and tell you that you can." I gave him my word, but I really didn't think too much of it. I was barely nineteen and wasn't sure if I even wanted another baby; especially after all the trauma we went through with this one. It took a few years to pay off the debt but, finally, that chapter in our life was over. And we had a beautiful daughter.

"And they twain shall be one"

Therefore shall a man leave his father and mother and cleave unto his wife and they twain shall be one flesh.

10 | I AM HEALED!

In February of 1987, Phillip took a fever. Shortly after a lump had formed in his throat and his jaws locked. He couldn't talk and was not able to eat or drink anything and soon became too weak to get out of bed. During this time, we had a wood burning heater. It was a challenge for me to keep enough wood in the heater to warm the entire house. So, I decided to move Phillip into the living room where there was a hide-a-bed. Shelly, our two-year-old and I slept in there with him. Brother Dillard Holloway, our pastor, would come every day and pray for Phillip. He always left us with encouraging words, and I was so grateful he did. Phillip grew up trusting God, so it was just another trial for him. Because I was still trying to obtain faith, this was extremely difficult for me.

One evening, around midnight, Shelly and I were fast asleep. Phillip was just lying there, praying in his heart, when suddenly a black image appeared in the corner of the room. He could only see it from the waste up. He said, "When I looked into its eyes the darkness was never ending. It was looking down on me and never said a word. It was death coming to claim me. I wasn't able to speak out loud. I said within myself, "Now I will know if I have God in my heart or just in my mind." At this moment, my heart is all that I can speak with. Now I know how Hannah, in the bible, must have felt when she was not able to speak. But only moved her lips."

As he laid there, feeling helpless, a voice spoke out of him. The voice said, "You can't have him until I turn him a loose." At that moment, the black evil image disappeared. Phillip was relieved and humbled at the fact that God was so attentive to him, in his moment of desperation. Our Pastor, Brother Holloway, and his daughter, Sister Wanda, had a nursing home ministry. They so faithfully shared the love of God with the elderly. On that Thursday afternoon, on their way to the nursing home, they came by and prayed for Phillip once again. Shortly after they had left, I was in the kitchen cooking dinner for Shelly and me, when suddenly, the smell of rotten eggs filled the room! The lump in Phillip's throat had burst. He immediately jumped out of bed, ran to the door and threw up. His jaws unlocked, and he then exclaimed! I AM HEALED! Once again God had come through.

Sister Temple, from Rayville, heard that Phillip was sick. She and her son Jay, drove up to Lecompte to see about him. Phillip shared with her his encounter with the illness and the spirit of death that he saw. He then proclaimed, "But last night the Lord healed me." She was relieved that Brother Phillip was ok. She then asked, "Will you come to Rayville and preach us a revival?" Brother Phillip was still very weak but never passed up an opportunity to preach. Soon we loaded up and drove to Rayville, Louisiana.

The oxidation pond

One day during this revival, a couple who attended the church there Johnny and Lonnie, invited us to their home for lunch. After lunch Shelly, our two-year-old wanted to go outside and play with the neighbor's little boy, Jeremy. He was five years old. It had rained earlier that day leaving a few mud holes in the yard. I informed Shelly that she was not to play in the mud. Jeremy assured me that he would watch her, and they would not get in the water. Just to be safe, periodically, I would take a look out the window to check on them. I was just about to go look again when Jeremy came running in with a panic. Shelly fell in the hole. I thought he meant the mud hole out front. I didn't know they had an oxidation pond; it is a pond that the sewer runs into, located behind their house.

Johnny, knowing what Jeremy meant, immediately jumped up and ran outside. I still wasn't sure what was going on, but we all ran right behind him. I was devastated when I saw her in that green slimy pond. It was five feet deep and well over her head. There was a post 8 ft. out in the pond, standing three foot above the water. Somehow, Shelly managed to get to the pole, but it was covered with green slime making it difficult to hang on to. Every time she reached to get higher on the pole, her head would sink right back into the water. Johnny, jumped right into the nasty stinky water before anyone else could get there and pulled her out to safety. She was traumatized, of course. But she was ok. I am so thankful that God was watching over her that day. I battled a long time with guilt. I felt that I should have been watching her more closely.

Years later, when our second daughter was two years old, we were taking a mission's trip to Jamaica. It was adults only. We decided to leave the girls with my sister-in-law.

After arriving in Jamaica, I was standing on the balcony of our hotel looking across that vast body of water that was separating me from my girls. A terrible feeling came over me the thought that something could happen to them, and I would not be there to protect them. I was perplexed. But then God, in a still small voice spoke to my heart and said, "You are not the one who watches over them, I am." A peace came over me. In that moment, I realized something bad can happen to my children right before my eyes, and I would not be able to prevent it. Because ultimately God protects them.

11 | THE MEASURE OF FAITH

During the early years of our marriage, I was so young and unfamiliar with faith. I would search and try to learn all I could about trusting God. I needed this faith not only for my walk with Him but also for healing. It seemed that everyone around me was trusting God for their healing. I would often wonder what would happen to me if I did not obtain the faith to do so. Will God honor my prayers and love me the same as He does them? well, I have grown a lot. I have not perfected my faith in God, but have learned that God is faithful. He's not just to a certain group of people, but to all who love Him. God is a mystery, and His ways are past finding out. We cannot create a formula that will make God love us more than someone else; He is so much bigger than that. It Is for this reason there is faith, and it is the only real way to see Him. To every man is given a measure of faith. Even if you don't feel like you are a man or woman of faith, you are! If you will begin to exercise that faith, it will grow. Abraham, in the beginning didn't have the faith to be what God intended him to be. Through the hardships and struggles he faced, "he became" the father of faith.

Your struggles will be different from mine, and mine from yours. But just like God knew what Abraham needed to walk through to become the father of faith, He knows what each one of us need. Just listen to His voice and He will lead you. God will use circumstances of life to get you to where you need to be. He may use finances or sickness. The one thing He is working on is to increase your faith, that you, like Abraham, will become what He created you to be.

    I can't help but think about Phillip's dad, as I ponder these things. He had trusted God for his healing many years and was even raised from the dead, when he was a young man. In his later years he had to have open heart surgery, his gallbladder was removed, and his kidney's had failed. The problem with his kidneys caused him to depend on dialysis for nine years. Did that take away from his walk with the Lord? Did this mean he no longer had faith? It did not! He was the sweetest Christian and trusted God to take care of him, until the day he died.

    The book of Hebrews declares that some received their dead raised to life again and others died. So, were some of them greater Christians than the others? No! They were all in the faith chapter they were all equal in the kingdom.

    As I said before, "God is a mystery and His ways past finding out." He knows the way that I take. And no matter where in life I may be, if I keep my eyes set like a flint, and serve Him with my whole heart, He will take care of me.

12| "HAVE THE BABY AT HOME"

In January of 1989 we were holding a revival in north Louisiana. We had our little motor home parked beside the Pastor's house. Every morning, Phillip and I would rise early and pray. While I was in prayer that morning, nothing outstanding was happening, (no rocks breaking or earthquakes), but I heard a small voice in my heart say, "Have the baby at home". It was as if a mystery had been spoken to me; I didn't have any thought of being pregnant at the time. I didn't say anything to Phillip. I just pondered the thought in my heart. Only a few days after the prayer meeting, I was cooking breakfast when the smell of sausage and eggs made me sick. Phillip thought I had contacted a virus. I said to him, "No. I am pretty sure that I am pregnant." I didn't tell him what the Lord had spoken to me. This was different, and I was trying to sort it all out for myself before I shared this with him. I knew I had to be fully persuaded to do this, because I didn't know how he would react. I knew we would have to take a stand against mom, and anyone else who didn't agree.

So, over the next few months, I never told anyone. I just prayed and asked God to give me the faith and courage I needed. I was twenty-two years old. I was scared and surly felt alone. I knew I needed faith, but I wasn't sure how to achieve that kind of faith. I was confused to why God was asking me to do this. The doctor made it clear to me that I could not have a baby natural. Now that God was asking me to do it, I felt like God had put a death sentence over my head. I knew I was going to have to pray through to a place that even if I had to do this alone, I would be willing to do it. I needed God to be real to me, not just a thought or something preached or talked about. I had to have the confidence to know He spoke to me. I needed to have the courage to act on what He said. I had to be willing to surrender all that I was and what people will think of me, and obey what God said. I knew prayer could change things but even greater than that, I needed prayer to change me. Prayer gives God an open view to our hearts. It reveals our desires to Him. When I began to pray for the faith to obey God instead of trying to change God's mind, God then saw a heart desiring to obey Him. That is when He began to work on my behalf.

Over the years, (because I had my babies at home), people would say to me, "Oh, you have so much faith!" What they didn't realize was, at this time in my life, I was searching for faith. The thing that carried me through was prayer, and the desire to obey God; and over time this produced "faith." You win or lose through prayer; if you pray and pray until you get the victory then you win. If you stop short of the victory, then you lose.

Another battle to sort out was telling mom; she was going to be so upset with me and with Phillip. I knew she was going to think that Phillip is making me do this. The relationship between he and mom that he worked so hard for will be at risk. After three months of praying and seeking God, I made up my mind that I was going to obey God no matter what. I told Phillip what the Lord had spoken to me in prayer that morning. He took it better than I expected him to. He walked over, took me by both hands, and said, "If you want to trust the Lord, then we will do it together and we will not fear what others say or think about us."

Just A Girl, A Journey With God

It was a trying time.

As people began to hear about our decision, they began to try and talk me out of it. My mother, of course, was worried and upset. She could not understand what was going on with me. Her first words were, "I know this is Phillip's idea." I told her how that the Lord had spoken to me in prayer, but she could not except it. My mom wasn't the only who was worried. There were also many other people who thought I was losing my mind as well.

Sometimes doing what God wants you to do means standing alone. I knew this was different, but I had no doubt that God had spoken to me, and I was determined to be obedient to him. Thoughts of doubt and fear often came to me. But when I prayed God always encouraged me, and the voice I heard that morning in prayer was always ringing loud in my heart. With our first baby, we did everything to please my mother. And the only one who suffered from that was my husband and me. So, this time I am going to do what I know God wants me to do. The bible says it's better to obey God rather than man. Phillip and I have a family of our own; we want to be mature enough to raise that family in a way that is pleasing to God. That will not be possible if we fear what people will think of us.

I didn't have a midwife and had no idea where to find one. One day Phillip came to me and said, "God has given me the desire to deliver our baby. I believe, with that desire, He will give me the knowledge as well." He began to study a few books on midwifery and was ready and willing to do the job. I fully trusted him. This was unfamiliar territory, and we were so young. Looking back now I don't know how we found the courage to do it, it had to be God.

Phillip's parents lived in Alabama. They pastored a little church there for twenty-seven years. Periodically, we would drive our motor home over and spend time with them. We never wanted to live there but it was a good place to visit. Two months before the baby was due the Lord spoke to Phillip and said, "Have the baby in Alabama." Looking back, I am so glad he did, it was a refuge for me. I was five hundred miles away from a lot of people who didn't understand what I was doing.

My Mother-in-law, being the great woman of prayer that she was, encouraged me daily. She believed that God had spoken to me and that the Lord was going to take care of me. No doubt God put us there so I could draw strength from her during these last few months. Finally, I went into labor I thought since the Lord had spoken to me to have the baby at home, it would be a quick an easy delivery. Much to my surprise, it was a warfare. Phillip always assured me if I changed my mind, he would take me to the hospital. This was never an option for me. My labor started. The pain and contractions were coming, but I wasn't dilating. Hours and hours went by, and I was only at three centimeters. After about fifteen hours of labor, I started feeling nauseated. I would talk out of my head and then throw up green liquid. I did this three times over a period of twelve hours. I did not realize it at the time, but I had toxemia. I had so much fluid on my body. My fingers would come out of their joints, and Phillip would have to pop them back in place. I didn't know anything about toxemia back then. At this point, I knew something was wrong, but I had no idea what it was.

I was feeling defeated and confused about what was happening to me. Someone came to my bedside and said to me maybe the doctor was right maybe you really can't have a baby natural. I was at a crossroad. Would I believe what the doctor said, or would I believe the voice I heard in the prayer meeting that morning? The devil was on my shoulder telling me I didn't hear from God and that I was going to die. After some time of being beat down and discouraged. Nobody wanting to persuade me either way, and the silence was deafening. I knew this was a choice I had to make on my own.

As I laid there still and quite, I began to think on the stories in the bible. God told Abraham, "I will make you the father of many nations." But it did not come easy. Through much pain and discouragement, he obtained it. Then, there was Joseph. He had the dream that God was going to make him a ruler. This wasn't fulfilled the way he thought it would be, and it sure wasn't easy. As I began to meditate on these things, I then realized that just because God said to do this it didn't mean it was going to be easy. I wasn't going to let opposition stand in my way.

I proclaimed, out loud, that God did speak to me in that prayer meeting, and that I would have this baby at home. No matter how long the battle is, or how difficult it may be, I am going to obey God. I then announced, if any of you are afraid you are free to leave, but we are going to have a baby right here! I now had the confidence that God was going to see me through, and no matter what the problem may be, God was going to fix this for me. My mother lived in Louisiana and did not want to be involved. After the labor had taken so long, she decided to intervene. It was a long ten- hour drive for her. My sister Ann, and my Aunt Virginia, 'mom's sister' came along. Mom's plan was to get me to the hospital as fast as possible. It was around 11 pm. When they arrived in the small town of Ashland, Alabama. About eight miles away from where I was. Mom had never been here before so she got turned around and couldn't find us. This was before cell phones and google maps. It was not easy to get directions at that hour of the night, especial in that little country town. Finally, they passed a laundromat. There was a janitor there so, they stopped to ask for directions. Mom was very stressed. She felt that she needed to give an explanation to why she was asking for directions to Mellow Valley in the middle of the night. She explained, "My daughter is there having a baby at home, and I am going to take her to the hospital."

The man responded, "OH, you are talking about the Holloway girl." He continued to say,

"You don't have to worry about her. Most of this little town has been praying for her. She is going to be fine."

His words did not seem to console mom at all. She had a strong will and wanted things her way, but this was different. I wasn't doing this just because it was something I wanted to do, but I was obeying God. I must say, taking a stand against mom wasn't easy. I had been in labor thirty-four hours when she came into the room, I was weak and tired, but I was determined not to let it show. As I began to talk with her, I started to feel strength. The more I confessed to mom that I was going to do this, the better I began to feel. I continued, "Mom I am not going to the hospital. God spoke to me in prayer to have the baby at home. I am determined I will obey him."

She then said, "You are so stubborn!" I saw her spirit began to break. But what mom was seeing in me was not stubbornness, but a determination to obey God, and she realized she couldn't fight against it.

Just A Girl, A Journey With God

I said," Mom, God will take care of me as long as I am obedient to Him." And then I thanked her for being concerned. I wasn't mean or arrogant to her, but I had to take a stand. She gave me a hug and said, "I know God is watching over you." To my surprise she then said, "I am going to get a hotel room call me when the baby comes."

Amazingly, after driving five hundred miles, angry and ready to take things into her own hands, Mom then humbled down, got a hotel room, and waited. This was a miracle. God did something good for Mom that night. She was always respectful and kind to both Phillip and me after that. When you take a stand on God's behalf, you are not standing alone. I watched my mother melt like hot butter in the sun. People who know her knew that it was an unprecedented behavior for her. It wasn't me that caused her to melt it was the presence of God. Two hours after mom left to get a room, it was time for the baby to come. Finally! A beautiful baby girl. I began to feel relieved, but then I realized she was not crying. Someone said, "Come on baby girl breathe, she wasn't breathing! Just then, that same dreaded feeling of fear showed up again. It tried to take a hold of me as before. I knew God had not brought me this far to be defeated. I sat up in the bed, and laid hands on her, and we all began to pray. I then reminded God that I did what He asked me to do, and that I believed in His faithfulness. During the prayer she let out a little fretful cry. That was all I needed to hear.

After an hour or so the baby was settled and sleeping. While everything was calm and quite, I decided to rest. All of a sudden, I took a chill. At least that is what I thought it was. I was shaking all over and struggling to breathe. Phillip began to put blankets on me to stop the chills. By this time I was shaking so hard, we both realized that my body had went into shock. I felt as if I were dying! Phillip then acted on what he felt in his spirit to do. He laid his body on mine. He put his hands on my hands, and his feet on my feet. I know that doesn't sound like the right thing to do. It may seem peculiar for a man to put all his weight on a woman, who has just given birth to a baby, but he was being led by the Spirit. He then began to talk in my ear. I will never forget the sweet calm tone in his voice. The peace, that came over me as he began to speak, was surreal He said, "You are going to be fine. You are God's child, and He loves you. He's got this."

While he was still talking, I fell into a deep sleep. I only slept about twenty minutes. When I awoke, I was perfectly well. I felt strong and healthy. We are thankful for our second daughter, Patricia Ida Holloway. She weighed 7 lbs. and 8 oz. She was so beautiful.

And they twain shall be one

The love that we now share was put there by God himself. God said," and they both shall be one flesh." When I was young and still trying to learn all I can about this wonderful life that God has given to me, I would often ask myself how can two people, that are so different, can be made one? Especially, with one of us knowing so much about God and a beautiful calling on their life, the other knowing nothing. Not even knowing if they have a calling. It was a mystery. How will God perform this miracle, and make two people one?

After facing mountains, crossing valleys, and walking together hand in hand, shoulder to shoulder, we now have a unity we never knew could exist. It wasn't until we had to learn to survive on our own that we realized how important it was to agree, as we walked together. Because our love for each other was so passionate, we began to protect one another. We fought off the adversary and always keeping a watchful eye.

    We faced, and continue to face, mountains too steep to climb alone. When one of us was feeling weak the other would be strong. We pulled each other along until we finally reached the top. The hardships coming so frequently, first to one of us then to the other. We are so busy protecting the person we love; we could not see what is happening. One day we realize there is a unity that can't be broken. A love that cannot be pulled apart by the storms of life. We are one and inseparable! We now have the same mind, and the same goals. With one heartbeat we serve the same God. Now, many years later, I understanding that the word "shall," is expressing the future tense. God was transforming us. We know that only through pressure, a diamond is born. Through our struggles and hardships God was transforming us into the "one" person that He had intended us to be. When God asks him to do something, I agree. Likewise when God speaks to me, Phillip agrees. We can now serve the Lord in unity. We are one and unstoppable.

13| PNEUMONIA

When Shelly was five years old, and Ida just barely six months, we were evangelizing full time and loving it. We had just finished a few revivals and were waiting for our next preaching engagement. Our pastors who were also Phillip's aunt and uncle, asked us to please park our motor home at the church until our next meeting. They said they wanted to be a blessing to us.

We had only been there for a few days when, death came knocking at my door. It started out just an ordinary day. I was feeling fine. I didn't have a cold and wasn't feeling sick in anyway. Phillip had gone to Lecompte to get something from the store and the babies were taking a nap. I decided to take a shower and wash my hair. Just as I had finished getting dressed, I heard a knock on the door. I went to the door, and it was Phillip's cousin, Donnie. He explained how he needed to borrow a tool and was wondering when Phillip would be home. I remember telling him that he had went to Lecompte and should be back any minute. Just then I passed out. Right in Donnie's arms! Donnie, shocked and confused, carried me to his mother's house, which was right behind the church. I was a lot smaller then and he must have been strong. His mother saw him carrying my unconscious body down that long driveway and opened the door and told him to put me in her bed. When I was settled, she then enquired to what had happened. He explained the dilemma; she then sent him back to retrieve the babies.

As he approaches the Winnebago, Phillip arrived from

town. He explained everything that had happened to Phillip. They got the babies and came to the pastor's house. As I said before, I was not feeling sick in any way. I do remember hearing mother talk about someone she knew that had just fell sick, and I never knew what she meant. That day it hit me so sudden. I had no idea I was sick, until I passed out. When I regained consciousness, I was burning up with fever. I was too weak to even get out of bed. I don't remember a lot of what happened over the next few days. Most of the time I was unconscious. I would wake up to take a sip of water and then fall right back to sleep.

Our pastor's wife, Sister Janet Holloway, put a mattress on the floor in her living room. This would be where she and my two babies, would sleep for the next several nights. I am so grateful for people like her, who are willing to sacrifice to help someone in need. They really didn't know what was wrong with me. At the time, they were pretty sure it was pneumonia. They knew I always trusted God for my healing, and they were willing to stand with me. Finally, after four days, the fever would break. Unfortunately, it would come right back. I remember feeling so discouraged. I felt like I was climbing out of a hole, and then falling right back in again. On the fifth evening, as I was alone in the room, I began to pray. I ask God to have mercy on me. I remember praying, "God, I want to raise my babies and be a wife to my husband, but I need you to touch me." Suddenly, it was as if God had revealed a secret room in my heart. I saw bitterness, that I didn't even know I had. Instantly, my mind went to a series of events, where a certain person had done hurtful things to me. A person, that we fellowship with quiet often, had wronged me in some ways. I knew I had some feelings of anger to some extent, but I didn't realize it had grown roots in my heart.

Here I am just twenty-four years old. I feel like I am dying, and I need a miracle. But all I could see was that ugly root of bitterness growing in my heart. God gently spoke to me and said, "Remove this bitterness, and I will heal you." Without delay I repented and removed the bitter feelings. From that hour I began to heal.

That person never changed. They still said hurtful things to me and talked about me behind my back, but I had changed. I never saw that person in the same way, after that. I realized they had issues that needed attention. Until this person is willing to deal with themselves, it would always be this way. But I had moved forward into peace.

I think this is what Jesus was talking about when He said, "forgive a person seven times seventy (490) times a day." They are not going to stop being who they are, but you can reach a place in God that forgiveness is a constant companion. And you will be able to see people like this from a different perspective. Instead of seeing there dominating spirit, you will see their weakness. You will have compassion on their hurting soul.

Over the next few days, I coughed some terrible stuff out of my lungs. My strength slowly returned, and I was finally strong enough to take my children home. Thank God I was healed!

14| THE CHALLENGE OF FORGIVENESS

I really can't talk about forgiveness without talking about Joseph. Joseph was called for one purpose at a young age, and it was to preserve his family during the famine. Unfortunately, when he began to share his dreams and feelings that God had given him, it only caused hate to arise in his brothers. This eventually caused then to desire to kill him. They appeased themselves by selling him. I can only imagine the feelings of hate and betrayal that came to Joseph daily. I'm sure the loneliness was unbearable. I can't imagine the grief he felt not being with his baby brother, which was his only full brother, (the others were his half-brothers) and his father, who loved him so dearly.

Night after night, as Joseph laid there in that foreign country so far from home, oh, the hate that must have swelled up inside of him for his stepbrothers. And even though Joseph did nothing wrong, he was the one that God expected to show forgiveness first. God had a calling on Joseph's life. In order to fulfill that call, he had to have a pure heart. He had to face hatred, betrayal, and loneliness. Being able to conquer all of this, made him the vessel God was looking for. When he finally saw his brothers again, instead of vengeance towards them, he was ready to forgive them. His heart yearned to let his brothers know that he loved them. It was at that moment, Joseph realized that the betrayal was God's plan all along. God was preparing him to preserve his family. I believe, if he had to do it all over again, he wouldn't change a thing.

Forgiveness has been most challenging for me. I feel sometimes if I forgive it will make me vulnerable and give that person the opportunity to do it again. I think maybe if I keep a little animosity between us, it will be a protection to me. And there is that little voice way down inside that says, "it wasn't all me. They need to forgive as well. If they are not willing to ask for forgiveness neither am I." This is a game that the mind will play. If you don't learn to silence it, you will never be able to move forward in God.

Trust issues can cause problems. I have been guilty of saying, "I forgive them, but I will never trust them again." I think trust is the biggest factor in forgiving. Especially, if this person is a vital part of your life. If you are not willing to forgive and to trust them, then you are setting yourself up for heart ache. It will form a wall in front of you and moving forward will soon become impossible. I know how hard it is to take that chance and trust again. True forgiveness will give you the courage to do it. Another hurdle is the desire to make that person pay for the wrong they have done to you; this is definitely a stumbling block. When you have forgiven someone, it is all behind you. That person has a clean slate, and they owe you nothing.

Forgiveness is letting go. Letting go of your fear that it will happen again and the feelings of hurt and betrayal. There must be a death to the part of you that wants to hang on to the grim thoughts, that are meant to haunt you. When a loved one dies, we have a service for them. A wake, funeral, "or" memorial service something to bring closure. It is the same with forgiveness. Especially if it is a daunting situation. You may have to find a way to bring closure before you are completely free. I have read that some people put their feelings in a box and bury it. They have a private service and walk away, leaving it all behind. For me, I find that when I realize

I need to forgive someone, I must first understand that I am the one that is guilty at this moment. No, I didn't do the wrong but I am the one trying to move forward in God, so I must deal with myself first. And for that to happen, I must repent to God for the bitterness in my heart, and then ask God for the grace to see that person the way He sees them. Unforgiveness must be replaced with love. If we can see that person the way God does, we will most likely see the woman at the well, or maybe the woman caught in the very act of adultery. We will see their weakness instead of their dominating spirit. The work of the spirit is forgiveness but without God's help and grace, this can never be achieved. Forgiveness is too great for the natural human to do on their own; it is a work of God almighty. But if we ask Him, it is His desire to impart this ability to us and we can be the vessel God is looking for.

THE NAIL

I want to tell you of an incident that happened to me. I love this story because it describes the work of the Spirit. The Spirit searches all things. The Spirit is the Evangelist of our soul. If we are willing to listen, it will lead us into all truth. First let me explain how the blood in our body works. It makes a complete cycle every forty-five seconds and has many jobs. There is one in particular I want to talk about, in this story. While it is traveling through the body, it is searching for impurities. When it finds something that doesn't belong, it will attack. It begins a process to remove it from the body.

As Phillip and I were cleaning our yard, one beautiful summer day, I had the push mower. Phillip was using the weed eater. As I was going along the fence line, there was a little pile of ashes. Someone had burned some old wood a few years before.

Bonetta Holloway

The grass had started to overgrow it so, I just pushed the mower right through it. When I did, a large nail flew out from under the mower and went into my upper arm, just above my elbow. It had been in the burn pile a long time and was very rusty. I never even thought about going to the E.R. I just went over to Phillip and told him to pull the nail out of my arm. So, he did. Rebekah, our baby daughter, was a teenager and still at home. She insisted I let her try to clean it and remove any visible dirt. She went to great lengths to make sure it was clean. She flushed the open wound with peroxide. She then had her brothers help her open the wound as wide as possible, and she ran clear water through it. Rebekah then put Neosporin on it and a bandage. In a couple of weeks, it was healed.

But three weeks later, the arm began to get infected. It was swollen and very painful. Eventually, it came to a head and a little piece of rust came out. I was relieved and was sure it would be fine now. Unfortunately, it wasn't long until it happened again. This time, I ran fever and was sick. After a few days it came to a head again. Sure enough, there was another piece of rust. Now, instead of one scar on my arm I have three. Even though Rebekah tried her best, she was not able to remove all the impurities from the beginning. But the blood in my body was doing its job. It kept searching and dealing with the problem until it completely rid my body of the little pieces of rust. In the same way the Spirit will search our hearts for impurities. When it finds it, rather it be unforgiveness or some other hinderance, it will keep bring it up until we deal with it and get it out.

Forgiveness is important in your walk with God, as well as your relationship with others. We must practice forgiveness daily. Peter asked Jesus, "How many times in a day should I forgive my brother when he sins against me." Jesus said," Seven times seventy." The religious leaders taught that you need to forgive only three times a day. Jesus, however, raised the number so high that He removed all the limits. Forgiveness is not to be given out in a limited fashion but in a measureless grace.

15 | A SHORT RECAP

Our two daughters were now nine and four. Even though we were immensely proud of them, Phillip really wanted a boy, someone to carry on the Holloway name. Let me recap for a moment. Shelly was our first born and I had to have an unexpected c-section. This caused the hospital cost to triple, of which we had to pay upon delivery The doctor then informed me that I can never have a baby natural.

Four years later God spoke to me in a prayer meeting, before I knew I was pregnant. He said, "Have the baby at home." So now I must decide. Will I listen to the doctor or God? Of course, I am going to obey God. Now everyone thinks I have lost my mind and I feel like I haven't a friend in the world. I was in labor for thirty-six hard hours with toxemia. My concerned mother drove five hundred miles to take me to the hospital but changed her mind when she realized that I am determined to obey God.

And now Phillip wants to have another baby.

Finally, a boy!

Well, Phillip did get his heart's desire and we are expecting our third child. God did not tell me to have this baby at home. I wasn't sure what to do. When I told mom that I was pregnant, she said, "Well, I know you want to have this one at home too and that is fine with me. I know God is watching over you. You and the baby are in good hands." I then asked, "Mom would you like to assist us in the delivery." She replied, "I would love to be there, but I am too nervus. I would rather just wait at home until it's over." I then said, "Ok but if you change your mind, you are welcome to come." I knew that this was my answer. If mom had enough faith in me, to have this baby at home, then I did too.

Here I am getting ready for our third baby and our second home delivery. We were in our home in Lecompte, taking a break from the evangelistic field. I am trying to rest and prepare for the arrival of our new baby. And then one day the phone rings. It is a pastor from star city, Arkansas. He is wanting Phillip and me to come and hold a revival. Phillip began to explain to him that we are expecting our baby any day and have taken a few months off. The pastor began to weep and said, "Phillip, I really need help and I feel that you are the one I am supposed to get for this revival. I need you now." I could hear their conversation. We knew the pastor personally, so our hearts were touched by his desperation. But at the same time, I didn't feel like we were in a place that we could help him. I then gave Phillip "the look". The one that says, "be strong and hold your ground!" As Phillip kept trying to explain that we are in a situation that cannot be helped, the pastor then said, "So, your wife is having her baby at home; you are delivering it? "That's right," Phillip replied. I was caught by surprise when the pastor then said, "Just bring your wife and if she goes into labor, you can deliver it here." At this point, I knew he was desperate. We agreed years ago that we would never let anything stand in the way of ministry. So, I told Phillip, "Tell him we will come." Phillip looked at me like I had lost my mind. But I felt that we needed to go.

During this time, we were traveling in a three-quarter ton

pickup truck and a fifth wheel. The church there had a house next door for evangelist and offered that to us for this revival. We didn't have to bring the fifth wheel, but we still had to travel six hours in the three-quarter ton pickup truck. For many, that means nothing. Let me just say, that is the roughest ride you will ever take, especially at nine months pregnant. After a few hours into the trip, I felt it was going to be impossible. We started stopping every hour and I would get out and walk a bit. I had even more respect for the mother of Jesus after this. I know that three-quarter ton pickup was much like riding a donkey. After that terrible ride to the revival, I was now in hopes that I would have the baby in Star City so I wouldn't have to make that miserable ride back home. But I did not! Now I am eight days farther along than I was when I first made the trip.

    I know all of this may sound a little foolish. You see, Philip and I purposed early on in our marriage that we would always put ministry first, no matter how difficult it gets, we will not let circumstances, pain, or our own desires hinder the ministry that God has placed in our lives. On April 26, 1994, it was a beautiful spring morning. When I got out of bed and looked out my window the sun had just begun to rise. Phillip had already left for work, and it seemed that it will be another ordinary day. I was so tired, and this baby was taking its time to make its arrival into the world. I had waddled for months now. I thought the baby would have come two weeks ago. I had not seen a doctor, so I had no idea what was going on. I just wanted to have this baby! I had gained a ton of weight and felt like this could go on forever.

    I had tried everything that everyone had told me to do. I drank hot tea, soaked in a hot tub of water, and of course, walk, walk, walk, but if you could only imagine trying to walk when you are nine and a half months pregnant. As I turned my thoughts towards the day, thinking how I can encourage this baby that it was time for it to meet the world, I decided to take a break from all the old wives fables on how to induce labor. I just wanted to rest and wait. After getting dressed, I made my way to the kitchen to start breakfast for the girls and myself. As I am stirring around in the kitchen I feel some cramps, nothing serious. So, I just pushed it out of my mind. Afterall, cramps are common when you are nine months pregnant, along with a lot of other discomfort. But wait! An hour has passed, and contractions were starting. I was in labor! I was so excited!!

Finally, this baby has decided to come. I immediately called Phillip at work and without delay he was on his way home. Wanda, Phillip's cousin, lived next door and wanted to be a part of this exciting event. With her demanding job, she had made plans to be with me as much as possible and hope the baby would come during the evening or night hours so she could be with me. I called her that morning, before she left for work, to let her know I was in labor. She came right over to keep me company until Phillip could get home. She was then off to work, hoping that the baby would wait until she returned that afternoon. And then there was my dear friend Hilda.

Hilda was a mother figure to both Phillip and me. She had no experience in delivering babies and would be no absolute help. She was, however, a good Christian lady. I loved having her around me. She always had a calm spirit and no matter what was going on she knew how to make me feel safe and that everything was in control. She lived two hours away. I immediately rang her phone. "Hello," she said, as she picked up the phone. "Hilda, this is Bonetta. I wanted to let you know that I am in labor." She let out a big Praise the Lord!!" and exclaimed, "I am on my way!" It was a little less than two hours when sister Hilda pulled in the driveway. Now I feel like I am ready for whatever is ahead of us. By the time Hilda got there, the contractions were steady. She found a notebook and began to keep track. She was keeping up with every contraction how long it lasted, and how far apart they were. When Wanda got there that afternoon, Hilda had a full report on the labor written in her tablet.

    I didn't have toxemia this time and felt healthy, so I was sure everything would go smoothly. There was lots of excitement in the air, and we were ready to engage in this wonderful event. Around six o'clock that after noon the labor stopped. Nothing was happening. It was if the baby had changed its mind and decided not to come. I soaked in a hot tub of water but to no avail. We all took a long walk. Finally, around mid-night the contractions started back. Hilda took out her notepad and began to record it all again. The pains lasted through the night and most of the morning. They stopped again. By now I am feeling a little distraught. Why can't I have this baby? Around Two o'clock that afternoon, Hilda brings me the phone. "Someone wants to speak to you," she said. I replied, "Did you tell them I am having a baby and I don't want to talk right now." In a very comforting tone she said, "I did my sweet friend, but they insisted." I took the phone, and a lady began with. "Mrs. Holloway you don't know me. I don't know you either. My friend and I heard you were having your baby at home and was wondering if we could share the experience with you."

    I was a little shocked for a moment, then I asked her "Why are you interested in home delivery?" She said, "Well, we have been taking some midwifery training and would like some hands-on experience." Still a little confused I said, "Let me think about it." After making some inquiries to who they were, I realized some of Phillip's family knew them personally and gave them good recommendations. I called her back and told them they could come. So now we have Hilda, Wanda, the two midwives in training, Phillip, and me of course. The labor stayed on its weird schedule, starting, and stopping all through the second night. By the morning of the third day, I was exhausted and confused to why I could not have this baby.

Naturally, there were thoughts of fear and the concern that something was wrong. But other than not being able to stay in labor I felt fine. Hilda was a true confidant. I know she was worried and concerned that something had to be wrong, but she never let it show. She always kept a positive attitude and had encouraging words to say to me. By now, it had been fifty-four hours on this roller-coaster ride. And the labor had stopped again. It was lunch time so, I asked everyone to please go to my kitchen and cook a nice lunch. I wanted them to take a break. At this point, I needed time alone. But Hilda not willing to leave the room, picked up a book and said, "I'll just sit right here in the corner and read this book." I was fine with that; her intentions were pure. She wanted to be sure I was ok. As soon as the ladies had lunch ready, they brought Hilda and I a plate. I sat up in the bed and ate a couple of bites. I was so weary that I did not have an appetite. I handed Hilda my plate and decided to lie down and rest again. After about two minutes of lying there, something snapped. Just as if you would have snapped your fingers but much louder. Suddenly, Hilda raised her head, "What was that!" she exclaimed. Just as surprised as Hilda, I said, "I don't know! I then explained, "I didn't feel anything, it didn't hurt." We just sat there speechless for a minute, and then it happened!! It was as if something had taken over my body and I didn't have any control over what was happening. Suddenly, I began to travail, my body went to work, and it was full speed ahead.

Phillip was right outside the room. He came rushing in with Wanda and the rest of the ladies right behind him. No one was sure of what had happened, but one thing we all knew was that the baby was coming. I was travailing so loud and steady. It never let up no breaks it was very dramatic. With all the pain and pressure, I didn't need anyone to tell me to push or breathe, my body was acting on its own. One of the midwives in training saw the trauma on my face. She looked just as scared as I did, but she got right in my face and with authority and sternness she said, "Don't be afraid! You are going to be just fine you hear me!!" She caught me by surprise, but it did calm me down a little. Even with all the travail and the women rushing around each other trying to get everything ready, I heard Phillip say, "I see the head." Minutes later it was over, and Phillip exclaimed, "It's a boy! Finally, at 4:05 that Friday afternoon laughter filled the room, and an excitement that was unexplainable some were laughing and others crying, but we were all thankful.

After a long and enduring wait and a mountain of concerns, and then an emotional and dramatic ending to this labor, the victory has come. In a special and unforgettable way, it was a great victory! I heard my baby cry for the first time. His cry was loud and strong. After a few minutes they handed him to me. There is nothing like holding your baby for the first time. He is perfect. A beautiful gift from God. I could hardly believe that such a miracle had taken place. In a short fifteen minutes I went from no pain to giving birth to a baby boy weighing 10.6 pounds and 23 inches long. Finally, everyone had calmed down, just then my mom walked up to my bed. "Mom" I exclaimed. "I didn't know you were here." She said, "I decided to come by and see what was taking so long; and you were having the baby. It was like God had orchestrated the whole thing so she could share this wonderful experience of life with us. We enjoyed the midwives in training; they had wonderful personalities and were very passionate about midwifery. They shared a few of their techniques with us and we shared some of our experiences with them.

If somehow, I had to walk through this again, I would never trust anyone else the way I have trusted Phillip. He never hesitated to step up and deliver those babies. He was calm, confident, and made me feel safe. He really believed in me, and I trusted him. I find it a great honor to have been able to engage upon this beautiful journey of life together with him and to embrace the experiences of family firsthand.

16 | SCHOOL DAYS

By the time I was ten years old, my two older sisters were married, and Mom and Dad both worked a fulltime job. Dad would leave for work at four in the morning, and Mom would leave at six. Before mom would leave for work, she would wake my siblings and me for school. We would get up and get dressed. Even though Andy and Kent were a little older than Clifton and I, it was my responsibility to fix breakfast for everyone, because I was the girl. It was always butter toast for me, but my brothers wanted mayonnaise toast. I do not know where this creation came from, but it was gross. All you had to do was spread mayonnaise on the bread, put it under the broiler oven, toast it, and you had the worst smell in the world.

We would walk down the long driveway and wait for the bus. But more times than not, when that big yellow bus would come to a stop, and those doors would open wide, with one accord, the four of us would take off running into the woods. Living in the country was so much fun. We were always getting into trouble, but we made so many wonderful childhood memories. Soon, running from the bus became a regular event. We would roam those woods all day, fishing in the creek, and riding Shetland ponies bareback. We loved being free and having adventure. When mom would come home from work, she always seemed to know when we had run from the bus. I didn't realize it at the time, but we had become the talk of the town. She would pull a switch off the old peach tree and stripe us good. We would always tell her how sorry we were and promised we would never run from the bus again, and it was a true repentance at the time. It wasn't long before the desire to roam those woods would overtake us, and even though we had the intentions to go to school that day, when the door would open on that old yellow bus our feet wanted to run. The school laws were different then, and we took advantage of it. I finally quit completely when I was thirteen and I went to work with mom in the nursery.

SCHOOL DAYS AGAIN

Phillip and I had never discussed where our children would go to school. Since I did not pursue my education after I was married, I always just assumed they would go to public school. When Shelly was old enough to start kindergarten, I informed Phillip that I would go to the public school in town and enroll her there. To my surprise, he completely opposed the idea, and said, "Oh no, you are going to teach her at home." I was overwhelmed by the thought that her education was in my hands. I prayed and cried. I finally found the courage to except the challenge in front of me.

I'm not sure how but I learned about the Abeka curriculum. I ordered it months in advance so I could study it well enough to teach her. It was a great curriculum and she learned very well. I did finally pursue my education. Little did I know that teaching would be a long journey for me. Brother Phillip and I taught all six of our children at home. God is full of surprises, what an adventure it is serving the Lord!

17 | FINALLY, A SHORT AND SWEET DELIVERY

It was July 28, 1996, on a Sunday afternoon around 5 o'clock, I was getting dressed for our evening church service when my water broke. I was caught by surprise; I wasn't in any pain at this time. My sister, Ann, and Phillip's cousin, Wanda, were going to assist Phillip with the delivery, but I didn't want to call them to soon, because I had such a history of long labor. I waited until their church service was over before I told them I was in labor. By this time my labor was pretty far along. I didn't get excited, I expected it to last through the night, maybe even longer. So did Shelly, our eleven your old. She was waiting on the front porch for her Aunt Wanda to make her way across the lawn. She then saw the headlights of her aunt Ann as she is coming up the driveway.

As they approach the porch, Shelly exclaimed to them both," I hope you are ready for a long and enduring night." Shelly had already been anticipating, the long encounter of labor that comes with childbearing, for me at least. By the time they arrived I had been in labor for three hours. An hour later, everything was progressing so fast that I said to Phillip, "This is not normal, something is wrong!" With fear trying to bear its weight on me, my sister and Wanda kept assuring me that everything was perfectly normal. I needed to relax and just go with the labor. It wasn't but an hour later Ann excitedly announced, "It's a girl!" Finally, I had given birth without the long enduring labor and the fear and anxiety that I had faced before.

It was an honor to have my sister Ann and Phillip's cousin Wanda to assist us, it was quick and easy, with no stress. I proudly named our baby girl after my sister, Ann. Rebekah Ann Holloway weighed 8 pounds and 6 oz.

When our little Rebekah was eighteen months old, she took a fever. We were in a revival at Rayville, Louisiana. It was the week of Easter. During the spring, there is always a lot of rain. This week it was extreme. She took sick at the beginning of the week. At first it was just a little fever. I though she was just teething, so I didn't think too much of it. Then she began to lose her appetite and the fever became more persistent. By the end of the week, I realized it was serious and we needed a miracle.

Every night I would bundle her in a blanket and take her to the revival, in hopes that somewhere during the service she would be healed. On Saturday night, the revival had closed, and our baby was still very sick. We were not being ignorant or neglectful. We knew by the Spirit that we were supposed to trust God completely for this baby. All the doubts and fears were very real, the reality of how it could end was on the forefront of my mind day and night. The voices in the early hours of the morning that said, "You are a fool for taking a chance like this." I was young and scared. When you take a leap of faith to trust God for something, it does not eliminate the fear that comes with the circumstances that you are in.

Every time we would decide to take her to the E.R., God would say to Phillip, "Just trust me." On that Saturday morning, Rebekah was lying in my bed sleeping. I was sitting in the little rocking chair holding Caleb, who was only two months old at the time. I had gospel music playing quietly and was just meditating on God. I was so weary from the long battle that seemed would defeat us, just then the song, "Last Thread of Hope" came on the radio. I didn't voice it out loud but, in my heart, I said to God, "Lord, I feel that a thread of hope is all I have left." God spoke right back to me and said, "That is all you need." Instantly, I had the understanding that if you still have a connection with God, even if it is as thin as a piece of thread and you haven't completely given up, then that is enough.

There may be a mountain of fear and doubt surrounding you; your mind flooded with all the bad things that could happen. But if underneath all this confusion there is faith in God, then that is all you need. It doesn't take a lot of faith to get God's attention. Just the size of a mustard seed will do. Nehemiah was delivered from the mud pit with rotten rags, so, a thread of hope is strong enough to deliver you from whatever you are in.

The next morning was Easter Sunday. It had rained all week and was still raining. Phillip woke up at 5 a.m. to pray as he always did. We had prayed what seemed a thousand prayers for our baby girl, to no avail. That morning, as Phillip began to pray, he said, "God I am coming to you again today with a petition to heal my baby and I am believing that you have heard me." He said that was all he remembered when the Holy Ghost fell on that Easter Morning. The Resurrector walked into our lives and rebuked fear and death.

The next thing he remembered, Shelly, our oldest daughter, who was thirteen at the time, was standing right behind him praying fervently. When he looked to the back of the camper where Rebekah was, I was kneeling over her speaking in tongues. I don't even remember waking up. It was as if the Holy Ghost in me acted before my physical body was even awake. When I woke up, I was already leaning over her and praying in tongues. The Lord then spoke to Phillip and said, "Go lay hands on her and rebuke the fever, then command her lungs to take air, and for her stomach to take food." He did exactly that. And then Phillip heard the words, "She is in recovery."

The fever left that morning, but it took a few days before her appetite and strength came back. But she was healed! I learned something about healing that day. There are miracle healings and then there are progressive healing. God said, "She is in recovery." When Jesus healed Peter's mother-in-law of a fever, she immediately got up and ministered to them. Not only was the fever gone but her health was instantly restored. Rebekah was healed that morning, but she had to recover. I don't understand all the ways of God, but I do trust him.

18| CALEB

" Faithful- wholehearted- brave-" "Devotion to God"

Now here we are in this wonderful chapter of our lives. On February 10, 1998, at 9 a.m., we now have our second son, "Caleb Nathanial Holloway." He was healthy, weighing 9.2 lbs. Phillip was beyond excited to have another boy to carry on his name, but that is not all that he would do. Little did we know that God had placed a call on Caleb's life. He would be a third-generation minister in the Holloway family. What a sweet blessing he is to this family. He is our fifth child. With a growing family my heart is so full. By now I am in full mommy mode, and I am loving it! I, of course, had some wonderful help Shelly and Ida were like little mommies. They treated Rebekah and Caleb like live baby dolls.

Caleb was always a good baby, never crying unless he was hungry or wet. But when this sweet baby was fifteen months old, he faced something most unusual. We were at our home in Lecompte, Louisiana at this time. We had been to a fellowship meeting at church and were on our way home, when Caleb began to cry. I tried everything I could to console him, but nothing seemed to help. Phillip and I took turns walking and praying for him. Sometime around 3 a.m. he fell asleep, I ruled it as a tummy ache or something to that nature. But, a few weeks later it happened again. This wasn't just a little cry; it was loud and strong like, something was tormenting him. No matter where we were when it came on him, it was going to last for at least an hour or longer. I would try to go somewhere private until it was over. And then when it was over, he was right back to the sweet baby he was before. This happened over the next few months. One night Phillip said, "We are going to call fasting and prayer until this leaves him."

After a three day fast and seeking God for him, on a Friday night around 9 p.m. he started crying. Phillip then took him in his arms and began to walk and pray. After quite some time he then handed him to me, and I did the same. We continued this for hours, finally around 4 a.m. he fell asleep. Phillip and I were exhausted. We took him to our room, laid him in our bed right between us, our clothes on and everything, just hoping to get a few hours of rest. An hour or so later, we were awaken by a short cry, Phillip and I sat up in bed, still exhausted, but ready to fight through till the victory comes.

Just then, we realized that Caleb is still lying there asleep. The little cry had come from the living room. I then told Phillip, "In the short time that we were asleep, I dreamed that there was a short skinny old man, with his white hair all messed up. He had a stick over his shoulder with his belongings in it, (just like the old hobo's used long ago.) As he was leaving Caleb's room, he went straight through the living room, and out the front door. After he went out the door, I looked out the window to see where he was going. There sat an old yellow taxicab. As he got in the back seat, it drove away. Caleb was never bothered with that spirit again from that day forward!

It has always amazed me how that little frail old spirit, could torment Caleb and the whole family like it did. Then I read in Isaiah 14:16, "They that see thee shall narrowly look upon thee, and consider thee, saying: Is this the man that made the earth to tremble and did shake the kingdom?"

Sometimes I think we give the devil more credit than he deserves. When David stood before Goliath, he never called him a giant. He called him an uncircumcised philistine. David saw him as a defeated enemy, even before he ever picked up the first stone, despite the giant's great image. David knew how big his God was. If we would not have begun to fast, and pray, and fight against this spirit, it would have tormented Caleb indefinitely, and it would have opened the door for other things to attached themselves to him. Our children are worth fighting for! No matter the sacrifices we must make, they are worth it.

When Caleb was around five years old, he and the neighbors' kids would be playing in the yard. He would always tell them when they were doing wrong; they would get so angry and him. They eventually nicknamed him preacher. Then just a few years later when Caleb was ten, we were in a camp meeting in Saluda, South Carolina with Pastor Danny Swinnea, God called him to preach. He has a great gift in his life, and we are so very proud of him. I believe the devil new the calling that God had put on Caleb's life. He was trying to stop him, even when he was just a toddler.

19 | THE WALK

You may ask why God spoke to me to have my babies at home, and why we had such battles with healing and a host of other things. I have learned early in life, that I may not always understand, but I always trust. When we were children, we played the trust game with our friends. If you are not familiar with the game, it was quite simple. Our friends would stand behind us and we would fall straight back, trusting that they would catch us. Well, God is much more trustworthy than any friend we could have. When we fall into His trust, He will not fail. We may not understand it all; but we trust Him.

I believe all that we go through, in this life, is about the "walk." Our walk with the Lord is everything. God told Moses, take your shoes off. What was the purpose? Yes, the ground was holy. Did God want him to touch the Holiness of God? Maybe.

One Sunday morning our son-in-law, Brother Justin Wilson testified on this topic. It really opened my eyes. He said, "The importance of Moses taking his shoes off and his bare feet touching holy ground, was because of the walk that God was about to take him on." God was getting ready to take Moses on a journey to bring deliverance to his people. He needed to be touch by God's Holiness. For us to walk with God, in his Holiness, we need to be touched by God as well. But we must understand all of Moses' hardships and victories were for one thing; to prepare him for the children of Israel's deliverance out of Egypt.

We all have a purpose in life. We may not see clearly right now what it is, but we trust the "walk." For eighty years, Moses did not see or understand what God was doing through him. All he could see was a wasted life in Egypt, and simply settling down on the back side of the desert until he was eighty years old. But what Moses could not see is that everything he went through was about his "walk" with God.

People, friends, and family will not understand your "walk" with God. But if you make God the forefront of your life, even though you yourself don't understand it; you will trust.

20 | GOD SAID, "ONE MORE BABY"

I was home schooling three of our children. I had a toddler and a baby on my hip. We were traveling full time, so we were in a church service almost every night of the week. We were getting in the bed late every night and we had to rise early in the mornings. I made breakfast for everyone and got them dressed to start our busy day. It was then time for school for our three older children. We had to get started on their lessons early enough to be finished in time for dinner. We had to have time to get dressed for church as well. It was a daily challenge and I felt like I was racing against the clock. Some days it felt as though I was losing the race. It wasn't long until I was feeling overwhelmed. Phillip and I had talked about more children but now I'm having second thoughts. I knew how much he wanted a large family. He would often say he wanted twelve children. But after a long tiring day of school plus church every night, there was no way I would agree to twelve. I decided that I didn't want any more, five would be plenty. He tried to change my mind at first, but then as he began to notice all the daily task I had with the children, along with the ministry, he agreed that five would be enough.

No matter how busy things would get, I always tried to find time in my day for prayer. It was something I had established as a young Christian. I must admit, some days I had to make time. Some days it wasn't until the late- night hours before I could get alone with God. One day, in my prayer time, I felt like the Lord was bidding me to do something for Him. So, I began to tell Him in my prayer, "Lord I will do anything you ask me to do, and I will go anywhere you want me to go. Just tell me Lord what you want of me."

To my surprise, in a still small voice in my heart, He said, "I want you to have another baby." I must say it took the wind out of my sail. I was speechless. I just got up an acted as if I did not here what He said to me. For the next few weeks, my prayer was very brief. I wanted to make sure that He did not speak to my heart again. Shortly after this, we were in a revival in south Louisiana at Victory Tabernacle, with pastor Steve McQuiston. They had an Evangelist quarter attached to the back of the church. They invited us to stay there, instead of driving the bus down. We did.

Phillip would get up every morning at 5 a.m. and go to the church and pray. I could hear him through all the buildings and walls between us. I would lie there thinking how could it be possible for me to hear him through all these walls? I felt maybe I should join him in prayer, but I didn't want God to speak to me again. I would try to block him out. On the third morning Phillip went over at 5 a.m. to pray as usual, but at 5:30, he came back in the room where I was. "Is something wrong," I asked. He said, "The Lord spoke to me." I replied with a reluctant, "What did He say?" He then replied, "The Lord told me He has asked you to do something, and you refuse to do it."

I was astonished that God had told on me to my husband. I just looked at him for a moment then replied with "I can't believe it." Phillip was filled with curiosity. He knew that no matter how hard something might be for me, if God ask me to do it, I will obey him. He began to enquire to what God wanted me to do. At first, I wouldn't tell him, because I knew he would be on God's side. But finally, I told him what God had spoken in prayer that day. I said, "God wants me to have another baby." He replied with a joyful "Oh, that's not bad, that will be wonderful."

I answered in a frustrated tone, "Yes, for you it is nothing but for me it is a big deal."

It wasn't that I didn't want any more children. I felt like my plate was full. If I had any more children to take care of, I wouldn't be able to keep up with everything going on in our lives. But of course, I was obedient to the voice. Nine months later, we were in that same church Victory Tabernacle, with Pastor Steve McQuiston, attending his annual camp meeting. It was Wednesday night. Phillip was preaching when I went into labor. We had planned that if I was to go into labor during the camp meeting, we would just drive home; we were only two hours away. Pastor Steve asked us to please stay and have the baby there. They wanted to be a part of this wonderful occasion. Also, some of the preacher's wives, who were attending the camp meeting, asked if I could please stay because they could share in this blessed event as well. There was about a hundred and fifty people attending the camp meeting. I was a little nervus about all of it, but it worked out fine. I was in labor thirty-five hours. Finally, Joshua Steven Holloway was born on Friday, July 6th at 2 am, weighing 9.3 pounds. There was a small group of preacher's wives there with us during the delivery.

We had the name Joshua picked out, but we did not have a middle name. Since Pastor Steve wanted us to stay, there so they could be a part of this event, we decided to give him the middle name Steven after the pastor.

Bonetta Holloway

So, we now have six children, three boys and three girls. We are blessed beyond measure. Each one has a beautiful and unique personality. They are not perfect, but they love God and for me that is enough.

Raising children is not for the faint of heart. It is a daily challenge but a worthy one. I am thankful for all six children. Now that they are all married, we have twelve. Once again, Phillip got his heart's desire.

21 | PHILLIP PAUL, "THE SPIRIT OF FEAR"

From the time Phillip Paul was just a toddler he was very rambunctious. I only had girls until he came along, so it was a rude awakening when this little storm came into our lives. He could be out of sight in a heartbeat. And when he caught my head turned, he would be up a tree faster than a squirrel. I stayed in a panic all the time; always afraid he was going to get badly hurt. One morning when Ida was just a little girl, seven years old I believe, she came to me crying. "What is wrong I asked?" She said, "I had a dream last night." I just assumed it was a bad dream because she was crying. On the contrary, she was crying because the dream was from God. I asked her to share the dream with me and she said, "Last night I dreamed that Phillip Paul was in two great big hands." Instantly, I could just see our little blond headed boy cupped in two hands, much too large for him to escape from. Such a peace came over me. When he was 10 years old, he encountered a spirit of fear. This was so out of character for him, and it caught us by surprise. Phillip Paul was never afraid of anything and definitely not afraid of the dark.

We were in revival in Arcadia, Louisiana, with Pastor's Roy and Hilda Antee. It was near the end of the revival when we noticed that Phillip Paul was nervous. He didn't want to get out of our sight. Then after a few days he was afraid to go to sleep at night. I started to question him, "are you having bad dreams."

"No ma'am." He replied, "I am just afraid, and I don't

know why."

His daddy thought a strong hand of discipline might encourage him to put this behind him, but it did not. It was then that we realized this was not a small thing, it was a spirit that was tormenting him and overcoming it wasn't going to be easy for him. The revival had ended. I was in hopes that being home again would give him peace, but it didn't.

The three boys Caleb, Joshua and Phillip Paul shared a room right across the hall from Phillip and me. Phillip had built a triple bunk bed for them. Phillip Paul's bunk was on the top. I would try to convince him that he was in the safest place, right on the top. But it did not make any difference to him. One of us, Phillip or myself had to stay awake every night until Phillip Paul went to sleep. At night when we were all trying to go to sleep, he would call out.

"Mom are you awake?"

"Yes," I would reply.

This would go on for quiet sometime and I would be so tired from the day. After tending to all the children, school and all the other activities, I just wanted to go to sleep. But I would do my best to stay awake, until he would finally go to sleep. If by chance, I could not endure and would fall asleep before him, he would cry all night until he saw the light of day coming through his window. Phillip, desperate for God's help, began a fast along with prayer.

One day in prayer God spoke to Phillip and said, "Tell Phillip Paul to read his bible every night when he lies down to sleep." Phillip Paul did exactly as his dad instructed him. Every night he would read his bible until he fell asleep. When this fear had first came on Phillip Paul, he started sleeping with his light on. Caleb was not at all happy about it, but Phillip Paul had to have a light. It all ended on the fourth night, after he had started reading his Bible. Phillip awoke at 2 a.m. and decided he would check on Phillip Paul. When he got to their room, the light was off. Phillip turned the light on just to be sure everything was ok. Phillip Paul was sound asleep with his bible wrapped tightly in his arms. Finally, it was over. For many years after that, Phillip Paul never went to sleep without reading his bible. And he has never been faced with fear or ever slept with his light on again.

22| ALABAMA

The big blue bus we traveled in while evangelizing was such a blessing. So many beautiful memories were made in it. I was very content with how manageable everything was for me. Having a home away from home made it easy with the schooling and with the babies. Even though we were in church every night and in a different town every week, it was manageable. We had only been traveling in it for a few years before the Lord changed our mission.

In September of 2002, we were in Star City, Arkansas, preaching a revival. The Lord was moving in every service. The church was packed out with people hungry for God. Excitement was in the air and people were coming from all around to be a part of this wonderful move of God. Strangely, Phillip was miserable. Every day when he would go to the church to pray for his nightly sermon, he would have these feelings of being inadequate. He felt he was not doing what God was wanting him to do. Finally, he realized that God was wanting to make a change in his ministry. He began to seek God for direction in his life. Willing to do whatever God wanted him to, he began to surrender his will to God's will. It was at the end of that two-week revival in Star City, Arkansas, when God spoke to him and said, "Move to Alabama and build a church." He then showed him in a vision of what the building was to look like and where to put it.

Phillip left his prayer meeting that Thursday morning and made his way to the bus. The older children had just started their school lessons, and the younger children were eating breakfast. Everything was going in the usual routine of things when Phillip walked in. He asked that everyone stop what they were doing and give their full attention to him. Of course, we did. He continued to say, "God spoke to me this morning in my prayer meeting. He told me that I have a mission to do for him. I would love for all of you to come with me and we can do it together. If you refuse to come with me, I will have to do it alone." I couldn't imagine what God wanted him to do that I would not want to be a part of. He continued," While I was in prayer this morning God told me to move to Alabama and build a church and pastor it."

It was complete silence, for what seemed a long time. I'm sure it was only a few minutes. All our minds were racing, thinking of the sacrifices that we would have to make. Alabama was five hundred miles away. Shelly was fifteen and Ida had just turned eleven. They loved the churches that we were in fellowship with, and the friends they had made. Evangelizing gave them the opportunity to see their friends on a regular basis. Traveling was always exciting for them. Phillip and I had moved to Alabama when we were younger, but neither of us liked it. We decided that Alabama would never be home for us. He knew I would not be happy about this decision. He was actually a little disheartened himself. But we all trusted Phillip, and his walk with the Lord. We assured him we would go and put our whole heart into it.

When we are Going through changes in our life, it often brings fear. The unknown can convince even the most dedicated believer to see the worst in any situation. When our thoughts start running away with what could happen, the little word 'if 'can be so big. When this little word is dominating our thoughts, fear comes. We know that FEAR HAS NO FAITH. When fear is controlling our thoughts; it is impossible to believe. The first thing Jesus would tell his disciples was 'fear not'. First and foremost, in order to believe, this had to be taken care of. God had spoken this to Phillip. Our whole lives were about to change. With that change comes doubt, fear, and the thoughts of 'what if.'

After dealing with all the feelings of doubt and fear, for some time, God gave me a dream. It was as if I was in another world and people were walking to and fro, but I seemed to be invisible to them. Finally, I made eye contact with a man who was passing by. I stopped him and asked, "Can you tell me where I am?" He then smiled and replied," Come with me; I have something to show you." Without even taking a step, I appeared in front of this massive machine of gears. There were all sizes of them and there were a lot of them. Some of them were very tall, much taller than me, and others no bigger than my hand. Some fat, some slim, but they were all perfectly timed and running at a high rate of speed. I was terrified to be standing beside something so massive, especially at the rate of speed it was going. My thoughts were 'IF' just one little thing goes wrong it will all come apart and I will perish. With fear in my eyes, never saying a word, I looked over at the man who had brought me there. He, knowing my thoughts, looked straight into my eyes and said, "Fear not, the God you serve has all of this in control." A peace covered me, and I then awoke. As I was lying there thinking about what had just happened, I knew the phrase "the God you serve has all of this in control" meant my life in general. If we can come to the place to believe that God has everything in control. Then fear will have to give way to faith.

As we look at bible characters like David, Daniel, the three Hebrew boys, and many others. The bible says that they were men of like passion as we are. That means that just like us, they were subject to fear. The difference was there faith was greater than their fear. When fear becomes the lesser and faith the greater, then we see the possibilities. This doesn't mean that the feelings of fear won't come from time to time, but faith makes fear inoperative in our lives. It gives God full preeminence. Despite the impossibilities, He gives us the power to believe. Only one can rule, if faith is in action, then fear has no power. If fear is ruling, then faith is dormant.

Daniel, ready to face the den of lions, with his heart pounding out of his chest and knowing what the end could be. He trusted that God was in control and whatever happened was God's plan for his life. The Hebrew boys when they said, "Even if God doesn't deliver us out of your hands oh king, we will not bow." Faith was greater than fear. They believed God was present with them and whatever he decided to do was good enough for them. When you fear God more than the circumstances, then faith is automatic. When God told Abraham to offer Isaac, Abraham was more afraid not to obey God than he was to go through with it.

Phillip began to share with us how the church was to set on the same property where his dad had built a small church twenty-six years before. Two years prior to this, Phillip's mother had passed away. His dad grieved so much that his health began to fail. He then had open heart surgery, his gallbladder removed, and his failing kidney's left him on dialysis. All of these hardships caused him to close the church.

The house that his parents had lived in for twenty-six years was also on the same property. Willard, Phillip's dad, was living alone since his wife had passed. Phillip's sister, Pat, had moved in with him for several months. But with other obligations, she was thankful that we were willing to move in with him and be his caretaker. I am so thankful for this special time in our life. Willard loved our children and taught them so many things. He was a blessing in many ways. Despite his age, and the dialysis three times a week, he lived nine years after we moved to Alabama. The house was a hundred years old, but still very sturdy. For many years it was only Willard and his wife living in that big ole' house. They only used a few rooms and it worked well for them. But we have six children so, now a remodel was necessary to make it functional for us.

Phillip's parents were wonderful Godly people and were always a great inspiration to me. Mildred had treated me as if I were her own child. She always took time to teach me the things I needed to know and pray with me. I will always hold her dear to my heart. One of the things I so loved about them was that they were old school. They always raised a big garden and canned their vegetables. His mother also cooked on a wood burning stove just because she enjoyed the experience. I can so vividly remember how wonderful those beans and corn bread tasted. She could fry okra like none other; her biscuits were to die for. She also used an old-time wringer washer for her laundry. Even though all of that was still in use when we moved there, I knew I would never conquer that wood burning stove. I can admire and respect people who can embrace this kind of lifestyle, but I wasn't prepared to do it myself. I couldn't imagine trying to keep up with laundry, on a wringer washer with six children. Not to mention cooking dinner on the wood burning stove. I'm sure it would not end well. I told Phillip, "I will go with you, but we will have to meet in the middle. There will have to be some changes in the living conditions." He assured me that as soon as possible, he would provide me with the things I needed to live a comfortable life there.

Just A Girl, A Journey With God

It was early November when we moved to the beautiful state of Alabama. We are located near Cheaha Mountain in the north-central area; it is the highest point in Alabama. The country is beautiful here, with its rolling hills and hardwood timber, making it a gorgeous place in the fall of the year. But it is also very cold in the winter. That big old house with its high ceilings and no insolation made it impossible to heat. We knew we didn't have the time we needed to do the remodel before the cold winter set in. Phillip began to search for idea's and found that the house had a large attic. So, we decided to enclose two rooms up there for bedrooms.

Phillip went to work right away to get it completed before the cold winds began to blow. He put plenty of insolation, sheetrock on the walls, and a thick carpet on the floor. It was very cozy and easy to heat. It was a little small, but we were able to be together and stay warm. Soon the cold winds began to blow. By early January, we had freezing rain and the temperature was in single digits. Everything stayed frozen for three solid weeks. It was one of the worst winters they had here in a few years. The house did not have city water. Instead, there was a water well in the front yard. The pipes where not properly rapped, so, the water in the house had frozen solid. Phillip was finally able to thaw one outside faucet. Which meant we had to go outside, in the freezing weather, every time we needed water, for the duration of the ice storm.

The children hardly left the attic at all during that winter. It got to be a little crazy before it was all over. With everyone beginning to think that we may have made a big mistake by making this move, I decided to find some entertainment of some kind. We had never owned a T.V. It was something we did not want to raise our children with, but due to the circumstances Phillip allowed me to get a monitor and a DVD player. I bought a few veggie tale movies. Finding Nemo had just came out so, I bought that one too.

Joshua, during this time, was not quiet two years old. He fell in love with Nemo. He wanted to watch it every day and, two or three times. That was almost twenty years ago, and his siblings still complain about how much they had to watch Nemo during that winter. Our bedrooms, in the attic, were nice and warm but the kitchen downstairs had no heat, except for the wood burning stove of which I knew nothing about. I would put on plenty of warm clothes and go down to the kitchen. If I was lucky enough to get a fire going in the old wood burning stove, we would get a hot meal. Otherwise, it was cereal or sandwiches.

Though we were in the states, it felt like a mission field. Besides the challenge of the living conditions, there was also the burden of building the church. Phillip did not have a job and we had no credit. We had always paid cash for everything. If we didn't have the cash, we didn't buy it. So, we didn't have any credit established.

The church was to be a 40 x 100. I couldn't imagine how we would ever build that kind of building with no finances. A few churches had sent an offering to help on the building. We were able to start the foundation, but soon the cold winter rain stopped the process. We spent the winter fasting and praying for direction on how to make this project work. Phillip was willing to try and borrow the money if the Lord would permit. But every time he thought he would go to the bank and talk to them about it the Lord would say," Just trust me." As soon as the cold rain had stopped, and we were able to get back to work, people began to send offerings. Sometimes they would send $100's and sometimes $1000's but we never stopped working on the building.

There was a sweet couple from Liberty, Texas that we briefly met while holding a revival meeting there, Pifer and Debbie Lucas. Pifer worked at the post office there in Liberty and Debbie was a secretary at a local business. They retired the same year with plans to travel. They sold their beautiful home there in Liberty and bought a new diesel truck and a fifth wheel. When they heard we were building a church, they decided to come to Alabama and help us build before moving on with their life's plan. Every day, all of us were out there nailing and cutting boards. Working from daylight till dark. The Lucas family were such a blessing to us. Surely, they are two of the most selfless people I know. After the church had been completed, they decided to stay and make Alabama their home. Once we had finished building the church, the Lucas' bought a few acres of land and Phillip help them build a house on it. They have been faithful members and dear friends of our family for nearly twenty years now.

Phillip was a roofer by trade. He could do some carpentry but had never built a building before. Building a church was quite a challenge for him. There were many times during this project when he didn't know what to do but, when he would pray, God would always show him. He built the church without any hired help; God always gave him the knowledge he needed. In exactly one year, on November 1st, the building was finished. The only one thing left to do was to install the central units. It was a miracle! Looking back, I have no idea how we did it; every time we needed finances it always came. So many people caught the vision and supported the work.

Bonetta Holloway

We needed to purchase the units and have them installed, and this was going to cost $10,000 of which we did not have. Pifer and Debbie Lucas stepped up and insisted that we borrowed one of their credit cards so that we could get moved into the building. It was mid-November when we had our first service. We were so thankful and proud of what God had done!

With only our little congregation present, Phillip stood behind the pulpit and said, "Our final cost on this building is $10,000. I am believing that God is going to pay this off by December 31st." As I sat there and did the math, I was thinking does he realize that this is only six weeks away. I must admit I was feeling a little doubt, but I didn't dare voice it. I know how God has already worked the impossible! Putting a time limit on this large amount of money did scare me a little.

Phillip and the country singer, Marty Stuart, just happens to be good friends. Phillip and Marty met in a church service in 1988. Marty has always held Phillip as a man of God. He wrote a book called "Pilgrims, Sinners, Saints, and Prophets." He wrote a piece on Phillip and put his picture on the front cover of the book. They don't have the privilege of seeing each other very often but every once in a blue moon their paths will cross. One day, unexpectedly, Marty called Phillip and said that he was conducting a singing tour. He said that the Lord had spoken to him that the tithes from the tour was to go to our church. This was in the spring of 2003. Every month we would get a check from Marty. By mid-summer the tour was over and the tithes from Marty had stopped. We did not hear from Marty again until I went to the mailbox on December 31st. There was a check from Marty Stuart for $10,000. The exact amount we needed to pay off the church. So, in exactly one year we were not only able to complete the building, but it was also completely paid for. God is such an awesome God!

Sometimes, when I am discouraged, and the enemy is whispering in my ear that maybe we are out of the will of God. I just remind him how that no one but God could have put us here. The amazing way the church came together was nothing short of a miracle. I think the greatest peace in every trial is to know you are in the perfect will of God. As long as I am sure of that one thing, then nothing can bring me down.

We had six acres of land to raise our children on and having three boys that was a blessing. I must admit, when I first learned we were moving to Alabama, I was not at all happy about it. My whole life changed overnight and not all for the good it seemed. I would often say to Phillip," The only reason I am here is because I love you, and I love God!" The living conditions were a challenge. Between balancing schoolwork, taking care of the small children, and working on the church building with Phillip, and experiencing that first winter was a nightmare, honestly, I cried every day for a year.

One day it was as if scales had been removed from my eyes. For the first time, I saw the beautiful rolling hills with cattle grazing on them. The beautiful bubbling brooks wound through the hardwood timber with their beautiful fall foliage of red and orange. It was breath taking. It was then, I fell in love with Alabama. I can't imagine living anywhere else, not even in my native state Louisiana. I thought moving to Alabama would be a degrading lifestyle, especially with the primitive surroundings that I observed when we had first moved here. But the Lord has blessed us with more material things, since we have been here than any other time in our life. I know for a truth God will do exceedingly abundantly above all that we can ask or think. We have been blessed out of measure. I have learned just because you don't see what God has in store don't cut it short. Just trust him. He said, "My thoughts toward you are for good and not evil."

23| PHILLIP'S MEMORIES

It was just another night at church. Mother had dressed us up as she always did, and she and dad took us to that little "tar paper" church, at least that is what everyone called it. There were no boards on the outside walls just 30# black felt paper, and back in the day it was called "tar paper." I can so well remember Brother Holloway, dad's oldest brother. Brother Holloway was our uncle, but to mom and dad, first and foremost, he was our pastor. My parents never allowed us to call him Uncle Dillard. It was Brother Holloway instead, in honor of being the man of God in our life. I am grateful that my parents taught us to respect those who are called to watch after our souls.

I always sat right on the front row. All we had for pews were some old foldup theater chairs that came out of a movie house. They were worn out; which is how we got them. I was so small my body weight wasn't enough to hold them down, so, I would sort of fold up in them. One night, as I sat there dangling my feet, I began to listen to the sermon (which I very seldom did). That night something got my attention, and my heart was stirred. When he gave the altar call, I responded. I knelt at an old fashion altar and poured my heart out to God as only a seven-year-old could do. I didn't understand a lot about God and His salvation through His Son Jesus. But I knew to repent to Him, and the blood of His Son would cleanse me. So, I prayed, repented, and wept my way to God and when I got up from the altar, I knew I was saved. I knew in my heart that Jesus was my Savior and if I was to die that night I would go to heaven. This is one of the many memories I have as a young boy in that little "tar paper" church in Lecompte, Louisiana.

Before Pastor Dillard Holloway was saved, he played music in the honkytonks, and was a great mandolin player. But his little Baptist mother prayed for him faithfully, until he finally went to the Baptist church with her and gave his heart to God. One Sunday morning as the pastor was teaching, he skipped over Acts 2. Brother Holloway was intrigued to know why and when he enquired to why he had skipped Acts 2, his pastor then informed him, "That chapter," he said, "is talking about the Holy Ghost. That is not for the church today." Brother Holloway believed that the whole bible was for us. He began to study on the Holy Ghost.

This happened during the time when Brother Temple had come down in 1954. He had that wild story about his wife Sister Clara Temple when she spelled out Lecompte in a prophecy and God said, "Go south and look for Robert Brown." Even though it sounded a little far out, Brother Holloway believed him. They began to work together. Brother Temple would come every weekend and hold prayer meetings in Mr. Robert Browns home. They would not only teach about the Holy Ghost, but they also demonstrated it.

Finally, they were able to find a building in town to have church in. It had been partially burned but they were able to fix it enough to serve their purpose. When they lost that building Brother Holloway purchased some land two miles out of town, on Hwy 112. There they built a little church out of sawmill lumber and wrapped it with 30# black felt paper. It became known as the "tar paper" church. The Lord was calling Brother Dillard Holloway to pastor that little "tar paper" church, but he didn't feel that he could successfully pastor his kinfolk, which was a big part of the congregation. After refusing to obey God for some time he became very ill. He was admitted in the Veterans hospital in Alexandria, Louisiana. Even though he was a young man in his early thirties, he was so sick that some days he couldn't even feed himself. The doctors were not able to find anything wrong with him, but he was becoming more ill all the time.

Brother Holloway knew in his heart what God wanted him to do, but he thought surely, he could change God's mind. One day he was able to slowly take a walk down to the pond at the VA. hospital grounds. He sat there on a little park bench and began to talk to God. And it was there that he began to realize that God was not going to change his mind. His Spirit broke and he began to pray and submit to Gods will. He said, "God if you want me to pastor those people at that little church, I will do it. But you are going to have to help me." From that day on he began to heal, and in just a few days he was home. He obeyed the call, and he kept his promise to God. He pastored that church for thirty years.

It wasn't long before we outgrew that little church and Brother Holloway decided we needed to build a new one. Times were hard back then, and we didn't even have the money to finish the little "tar paper" church. One day a lady that lived a few houses down from the church, stopped by Brother Holloway's house. Though she had never attended any of our services, she said that she wanted to give a donation to the church. Her donation was $500. In the 50's that was a lot of money. Brother Holloway knew it was a sign that God was ready for him to build a new church. He began to build, and people came from everywhere to help not only with labor but monetary blessings as well. When we moved into our new church it was paid for. Brother Holloway was a wonderful man of God and one of the best teachers I had ever sat under.

On March 3rd of 1990, at age 62, our pastor Brother Dillard Holloway passed away from an aneurysm. There was not an assistant pastor. I was Evangelizing full time, preaching almost three hundred times a year. Sister Janet, (Brother Holloway's wife) asked me if I would fill in for a while, until they could work something out. I agreed to do it for a few weeks or so. But then, one day while in prayer, God spoke to me and said, "I will leave you here for a season." That season lasted four years and nine months. And then he gave me leave to Evangelize again.

The church is still there on Hwy 112, and has never deviated from the teachings it was founded on. And it still holds many wonderful memories, it is where God gave me my roots many years ago. I have considered many times over the years if Pastor Temple had not obeyed God. I wonder would we have found God in the fullness that we know him today.

Let me encourage you as a preacher of this great book, "the Bible," obey God because every person that obeys God adds another step to the stairs that leads to heaven. Notice the bible says, Abraham, Isaac, and Jacob. All three of these men had to obey God or Israel would not be here today. Your obedience is very important. What you do will affect generations.

When Pastor Temple prayed for my brother Robert as a baby and God healed him. It influenced my mother to serve God and that is what has made it possible for my grandchildren to know God. So, your decisions will not only affect you but those who will come behind you even years after you are gone.

NICARAGUA

It was the summer of 1974, less than one year after I was called to preach. I had just turned fifteen in March and had only been preaching for a few months when Pastor John Temple invited me to go to Nicaragua with him. Our home church supported pastor Temple as our Missionary. He had started our church in the 50's and after that became a missionary. God had given Pastor Temple a dream and told him to go to Managua, Nicaragua, and look for a man named Ralph Henry. He did and sure enough he found Ralph and his wife Ruby. They became his interpreters for many years, and lifelong friends. In June of 1974, I flew out of New Orleans and headed for a different country. I had no idea what I would be doing for the next month. The flights back in the day were not non-stop as they are now. First, we flew into Belize, then Tegucigalpa, then Managua, Nicaragua. There we met Ralph Henry Pastor Temples interpreter.

Ralph Henry was from Kukra Hill, but he had set up a three-day meeting there in Managua. He had made accommodation for us with a sweet family there in the city. Even though it was a city they didn't have indoor plumbing. Everyone had an outhouse. There was no place to take a bath and not even a private place to change clothes. The houses were made with one small open room then two small bedrooms. They had several children whose ages ranged from young teens to infants. With no other place to put us, we all stayed in the room with the children. I well remember the little boy who slept above me. He was sleeping on, what looked like a large inter tube that they had split open and had made a Hammack out of it. The last night that we were there I was awaken by a drip, drip, drip. It wasn't raining outside. It didn't take long to realize that he had wet the bed and I was in the line of fire. This only added to the smell of my clothes. I was already three days into wearing at the time.

Our church had purchased Pastor Temple a ¾ ton pickup truck there in Nicaragua. It was several hours away from Managua, so we caught a bus and headed that way. As we were leaving out of town another bus had just been raided. I saw the men with their machine guns as we approached the burning bus. I gave a sigh of relief when our bus driver pressed the gas and kept going. Now I am really wondering what I have gotten myself into. But after several hours we arrived in the little village where our truck was awaiting us. It was late by this time, so we had to stay the night with a family there.

Pastor Temple was helping Ralph Henry build a church in his little village there in Kukra Hill. So, the next morning we purchased twenty bags of concrete and loaded them in the truck. Mind you, we are all still wearing the clothes we left from home in. I am wondering why I even brought a suitcase. Still on our way to Kukra Hill, we arrived at a place called Rama. This was as far as we could go by land. We had to leave the truck and travel by boat. We had to load all that concrete onto a boat. That afternoon we unloaded the concrete from the boat, stayed the night, and took another boat the next day. So, yes, all the concrete had to go on that boat as well. Finally, we arrived at Kukra Hill. They had a couple of old trucks there to help families get their supplies from the river to their homes. We were able to use one of those trucks, we didn't care that it was not pretty, it smoked, and the front wheels wobbled as it rolled over the rocks. We were concerned whether it would make it up the hill to Ralph's home before dying for good. Well, it did make it and finally and we unloaded the concrete for the last time.

After the last sack of concrete was unloaded Pastor Temple said, "Let's go to the creek and take a bath." So, we grabbed our clothes and headed to the creek; it felt so refreshing to be clean again. One of the mothers there offered to wash my clothes and I graciously agreed, but, when I saw her beating my dress pants on the rocks at the creek, I was having second thoughts.

We stayed with Ralph and his wife Ruby for a few days. Ruby was a wonderful lady; Ralph was tall and slender, but Ruby was only 4 ½ feet tall and as round as a Maytag washer, but she was so anointed to preach. They lived in a two-story house and on the bottom floor, in the front room was where they gathered for church 365 days a year. Kukra Hill didn't have electricity, so, Ralph used an old power plant for enough electricity to have lights, and for Ruby's electric guitar. The old power plant was worn out and oil would get on the piston and foul out the plug ever night. Each day I would take the head off of it and clean the top of the piston and plug, being as careful as possible not to damage the head gasket, so, it would be ready for the next service.

Ralph had forty or so that showed up every night for church. When Ralph was away preaching Ruby would take over. She was a great preacher as well. I loved it when she would interpret for me; she was so anointed. Ralph and Ruby had taken in a little boy who was ten years old. His name was Alvear. I'm not sure what had happened to his parents, but they gave him a home. Alvear could speak three different languages and English was one of them. He had never gone to school for it. It was a gift. Alvear became my best friend, and I took him ever where I went. They had a sugar mill there in that little village. Sister Ruby had run out of sugar. She sent me and Alvear there to get a hundred pounds of sugar. I didn't even consider how I would get it home but after we made the purchase, they just threw it on my shoulders and said, "thank you." Back then I didn't weigh much more than a hundred pounds myself, but I did manage to make it all the way back home with it.

I was having a hard time eating all the beans. They had rice for breakfast and beans for lunch, then rice and beans for dinner. After several days of that my stomach began to swell. Finally, I told Alvear I wanted to buy some bananas. I felt that eating them instead of so many beans would help my stomach. So, Alvear took me to a man there on Kukra Hill. He only sold them by the stalk, and it was all I could do to carry them back to the house. I soon realized I had way too many, so, I shared them with the children next door. They would open their wooden window shutters and I would open mine, and I would throw them bananas.

It was our last day on Kukra Hill, when we got word that a little boy from another village had been bitten by a spider and died. The parents sent for Ralph and Pastor Temple to come and take care of the funeral. Pastor Temple asked me to come along, so, I did. There were no roads only trails to follow until we came to the little village. It was the middle of June, and the heat was almost unbearable. We could smell the little boy before we reached the house where the funeral was being conducted. It smelled so bad I could hardly stand it. It was quite an experience for a fifteen-year-old boy. When I was close enough to get a view there was no casket. The little boy was lying on a board, his mouth, and eyes wide open, and flies were everywhere. At that moment I became very grateful for America; we are so blessed here.

Just A Girl, A Journey With God

Ralph was so busy working on his church and though he was our interpreter, Pastor Temple didn't want to inconvenience him. So, Pastor Temple decided to visit an English-speaking town down the river called Pearl Lagoon. Pastor Temple and I, jumped on a boat and headed for Pearl Lagoon.

When we arrived at Pearl Lagoon the pastor then met us, his last name was Temple also. Their government was building new houses along the river in that little town, so, we had the privilege to stay in one of them while we were there. There were no beds, just a table and two chairs, no electricity, or bathrooms. It was beautiful there and everyone spoke English. They were also getting sewer and water for that community. But for now, it was candlelight and we had to bathe in the river. When I went to the river to take a bath, I noticed that their outhouses were hanging just over the river. I eased out of the water and waited to take my bath when I returned to Kukra Hill. That night when we sat down for dinner, the only light was a small candle in the center of the table. As we began to eat the food it was crunchy, and it really didn't have a taste. I couldn't see what it was, so I asked Brother Temple, "What are we eating?" he looked at me with a smile and said, "Fisheyes." It was at that moment I realized I was full and dismissed myself from the table.

The next day the Pastor took Pastor Temple and I down the river thirty minutes from Pearl Lagoon to another village on the riverbank. It was beginning to get dark by the time we reached the little village, the only light besides the moonlight was an old lantern hanging from the limb of a tree. There was a large crowd of people sitting and standing in the shadows. God moved mightily in that little village, and they were English speaking, so we didn't have to preach through an interpreter.

Bonetta Holloway

I was young in age and young in God, but it was most rewarding. Some days I preached three times a day, sometimes through an interpreter and sometimes not. God moved mightily among his people there in Nicaragua. I didn't know it at the time, but Pastor Temple saw the call on my life and took the time to take me to Nicaragua. It gave me experience and confidence. I will forever be grateful to him.

I have never had the opportunity to go back to Nicaragua, shortly after our trip Pastor Temple passed away and so did Ralph Henry, the interpreter. My mother and dad kept in touch with Ruby. They sent financial support to her. They would faithfully send candy to the children there at Ruby's church. Mom and Dad continued this until word came that Ruby had passed away.

Mission work is so rewarding. I encourage young men and women to take every opportunity to do so. I have preached in Nicaragua, Jamaica, Mexico, and Honduras. I wouldn't take back one thing that I have done for the kingdom of God.

24| REBEKAH'S MEMORIES

I can still remember riding in our big blue bus and listening to that diesel motor purr, as it would go down the highway. I'm not sure why my brothers and I thought it was so much fun to stick our heads out the window to make the big trucks blow, as they went by. One day, Caleb decided he wanted my spot. He pushed me out of the way, making my favorite Pacifier fly out of my mouth (which I shouldn't have had at the age of five anyway). I remember seeing that poor thing bouncing down the road. My heart sank, because mom had already informed me that when I lost this one there would not be another. I went from fun and friendly to how many hits can I get in before mom catches me. I was doing a pretty good job at defending my pacifier, until mom opened the door that divided the front of the bus from where we were. She said, "If I have to come back there it's not going to be good!" Knowing what that meant, I realized my sweet pap wasn't that important after all.

We had so much fun playing in the bus while we traveled the roads. Pillow fights, riding our little bikes from front to back, building forts, and then cleaning up as quickly as possible when dad announced that we were making a pit stop. And I always remembered to skip the bottom step when I would exit the bus; if I didn't it would shock the living daylights out of me.

When we made our big move to Alabama, where dad would be pastoring. I never realized how much I would miss our fun travels in that big ole bus. And little did I know, this move would be the beginning of a new adventure.

We now have four cousins living right next door, all boys of course to add to my three brothers. I am the only girl, so, I had to be tough to say the least. I remember papaw telling me, "It's either fight or die baby girl." So, I learned to fight. Don't get me wrong, I loved to cook and had a full play-doo kitchen. I would make the boys eat at my kitchen a lot. There were a few "girly" things that I liked to do, but I loved being outside; bikes, sports, guns, tree climbing etc. That is what most of my days consisted of, especially if I wanted someone to play with. Before we knew it, life got busy as dad began the work on the new church building. We had plenty of people around to help share the load. For me, at eight years old, it was school and then being adventurous with my brothers and cousins in the woods near the house.

When I was ten years old, I was playing in the woods with the boys one day. We loved to climb trees, I noticed that there was something growing on them, but I didn't think anything of it, until the next morning when my face was so swollen that I couldn't open my eyes. When mom saw my face, she knew that I had gotten into poison ivy in the woods. Unfortunately, I am very allergic to poison ivy. For the next few days, I looked like someone had beaten me in the face. Mom didn't even let me leave the house because she was afraid someone would call DHR. My hands were swollen so bad, they were bursting open and bleeding. I was broken out from head to toe and in so much pain. My little body was covered in way too much calamine lotion!

Daddy told me, right from the beginning, that he would take me to the E.R. He wanted me to make that decision for myself.

A few days later, I was setting on the front porch and thinking maybe I should see a doctor. But as I sat there, I began to think about mom and dad's life. How they trusted God for everything, and how I wanted that kind of faith. I had seen God come thru so many times for our family. I wanted to trust in God and be faithful to him like my parents did!

I decided to trust God. I didn't realize it at the time, but Dad was teaching me to make my own choices in God. But three days into it, I was getting worse. The thought crossed my mind that I should go to the hospital, but I really wanted to tough it out like momma and daddy would do! I didn't completely understand why they trusted God the way they did, but I wanted to find out what it was like for myself. The next morning, I was lying on the couch, wishing all of It would just go away. To be honest I was scared. Between the pain, swelling, and the mind battle, the hospital idea was sounding pretty good. I didn't tell anyone but every night I would go to sleep thinking that I wouldn't wake up the next morning. Finally, one day mom called dad at work and told him something had to happen. She was worried that the poison ivy was going to get into my eyes and cause me to go blind. She informed dad that either we had to get a miracle or see a doctor. Daddy told Mom, "Don't do anything, I am leaving work now and will be home soon." When dad got in the truck to head home, he started praying. Dad later told us that while he was driving home just as his tires hit the foot of a bridge that he was crossing the Holy Ghost spoke to him and said, "I am going to heal her!"

When daddy arrived home, he went next door to the church to get the anointing oil. Mom pulled the coffee table into the middle of the living room and sat me on it. When dad walked into the house he said, "You don't have to worry Rebekah, God said He is going to heal you." He then anointed me with oil and mom, dad and all my siblings began to pray. I didn't know that God had spoken to dad on his way home, but I had made my mind up, that no matter what happened I was going to trust God fully! The verse came to me "for God has not given us the spirit of fear, but of love, power, and a sound mind." while praying I told God that if He would heal me, I would never go to a doctor or take any medication out of fear for my life. I would trust him to keep me safe.

When I went to bed that night, I looked the same, but I had peace. The next morning, when I woke up, the swelling was gone. I looked like nothing had ever happened. I was so thankful and happy; simply for the fact that God heard my prayer, and He took the time to help me. As I have gotten older, and I have realized how dangerous the situation was I'm so thankful. God had His hand on my life and at ten years old, He instilled a faith in me that would carry me through so many battles and situations of life. Having faith is not always easy, and sometimes it may not make sense, but in the end, no one can take care of you or knows what you need better then God can!

As I entered my pre-teen years, I do believe one of my greatest battles was being nice. I was around seven mean boys all the time. I think that may have played a small part in it. I recall one time in particular, I was playing basketball. Jesse one of my cousins whom I would fight with a lot, decided to walk up, and hit me in the head with the basketball. He would then flee up a nearby tree so that I couldn't catch him. Laughing all the while, saying, "You can't get me." I was about to start up the tree to prove him wrong, when I realized dad's chain saw was lying there. It didn't have a chain on it, but Jesse didn't know that. Suddenly I had an idea! I looked up at Jesse with a smile and said, "Hey Jesse, I'm going to cut the tree down and then get you." I then started trying to crank the chainsaw and pretend to cut down the tree. The poor kid started down the tree so fast. After the second step, out came his feet from under him. I will never forget how he straddle those branches, before hitting the ground. By this time, I was laughing too hard to even make sure he was okay. Poor Jesse! He was lying there for a minute, trying to get a handle on the pain. He then jumped to his feet, red in the face, mad and hurt, pointed his finger at me and said, "Rebekah, you could have killed me!" Then he went running home shouting, "I'm going to tell my momma!" I then replied, "Go ahead I'll tell her you hit me with a basketball." I know what I did to him was much worse, but nothing could take that moment of revenge away from me.

As a few years passed we had so much fun. Sometimes it got us in trouble, but some of it we got away with. As I look back on all the good, bad, and ugly even when it was really hard for us, we were still a family who cared for each other, rather we wanted to admit it or not! Mom and Dad always somehow kept us close and taught us many valuable lessons along the way. They not only taught us but showed us how to respect others, always follow God no matter what everyone else said, and to have a personal walk with God.

1. You break it! You fix it! Even though you are young be responsible.

2. Always give the job 100%, even if there is no pay involved.

3. Never help someone looking for something in return. It's better

to give then to receive.

As I got older, I learned these were very important keys to life, and sooner than I thought, I would need them. I will never forget when On December 15th, mom received a call that daddy had fallen off a roof. He had already sent the other guy's home and was going to do a few finishing touches. It started to sleet, causing the metal roof to become impossible to stay on. His foot slipped, and he lost all control. Dad went sliding down the roof and flying off so fast he landed about 15 feet in the front yard. He had left his phone in his truck. He had to crawl to his truck and call the guys to come back and help him.

At the time, we didn't know how bad it was. We were worried to say the least. Mom called the local chiropractor. He had already closed for the day, but he agreed to meet them at his office to x-ray dad and check for any broken bones. Thankfully no bones were broken. His hip; however, was out and was swollen so badly that the chiropractor couldn't do anything for him, until the swelling had went down. I had never seen him in that kind of pain before. He never went to a doctor. The chiropractor started working with him after a few weeks. It was months before dad could do anything and one year before he could go back to work.

Mom and Dad had taught us well. We all began to pull together to make ends meet. Ida already had a job; Momma went to work at the Dollar General. Phillip Paul and Caleb were too young to take on the business at the time, but they were able to work for other roofers from time to time. I stayed home to watch after Joshua and take care of daddy. It was challenging for all of us, but we never thought twice about what we needed to do. As the months passed Daddy began to heal and before we knew it, things were getting back to normal.

In 2013, I reconnected with a guy from my childhood Daniel Sharpe. He was from Locust Grove, Georgia. I hadn't seen him since we were kids, but I had just turned sixteen, so we started to date. In June of 2015, he proposed, and I said "yes!" March 12, 2016, I married the love of my life. Together we started a new chapter in our lives. The first few years of our marriage, we had challenges. A lot of the time with very little money. But we had love, and most importantly we had God. We have learned how to love in the good and bad. By God's help, we have learned how to settle our differences without an all-out fight. Of course, we have disagreements, but I saw my parents work through things without yelling and fighting. We purposed to do the same. People would tell us to give it time, the big fight was coming. But by God's grace, we have been able to resolve our differences peaceably.

I'm not going to say that it was always easy, but at the beginning of our marriage we talked about what we wanted from our relationship. Along the way we learned to establish these seven things in our marriage!

1. Always be open and honest.
2. Always keep God in the middle.
3. Sometimes I am wrong.
4. Pray to see their point of view, before you pray for God to change them. (It maybe you.)
5. Watch what you say, you can't take words back.
6. Talk it out like adults, no need to yell like children.
7. Always respect each other especially around people.

With lots of prayer and growth, God has truly helped us in

this, and blessed our marriage and I am so thankful!

When Daniel and I got married we was both aware that I may not be able to have children. Although we both wanted at least one child, Daniel said he would love me no matter what. Was that ever true! The end of September of 2017, to my surprise, we found out we were expecting. Later, Daniel told me that he had gotten a prayer cloth and kept believing that God would bless us with a baby. We were so happy to be starting a family. My pregnancy was one of the hardest things I had ever went through. The first few months, I lost 23 pounds from throwing up. I couldn't keep anything down. As the months passed, I went from passing out, to heart problems. From there what they thought was seizures, followed by EEGs, and many nights in the hospital.

After that came bed rest because the baby was trying to come at twenty-six weeks. The list went on and on. With doctors giving me very little help of understanding what was going on. I was scared for my child's life as well as mine. But one Sunday morning six- months into my pregnancy while setting in church, I passed out. As I began to regain consciousness, I could hear the prayer warriors around me. I could feel the power of God in the room. I will never forget the moment I felt healing flow through my body! Praise the Lord!!!

God could not have given me a better man then my husband; he was my rock through all of this. When I felt helpless, there was not a time that he was not there for me and our son. I can still smell chicken patties cooking in the microwave as he was preparing them for our supper. (Because that was all that he knew how to cook.) But he never complained: he would always hold me tight and say, "I will do whatever I have to, for my family." The last seven weeks was the easiest part of my pregnancy. Thinking back my poor momma spent more time in Georgia than she probably wanted to. I was really glad I had her there the last weeks, as she just patiently waited for her grandson to be born.

On June 4, 2018, at 11:04 pm at 9 pounds 4 oz 19 inches long, our sweet healthy son was born. Mathias Paul Sharpe, (which means humble gift from God) he was finally here, and we could not be more happy and grateful for this beautiful gift that God had blessed us with. After he was born, we felt that God was directing us to move to Alabama where we would be attending my parents' church.

This was a big change for Daniel. He had always lived in Georgia and had a job there that he really enjoyed. But God was asking him to leave his comfort zone and he did. We had been there a year when we bought a fixer upper. It was a single wide trailer that needed a lot of work; but we enjoyed the project until it came to a stop when Daniel had a terrible accident.

On the morning of August 26, 2019, Daniel and I were working on our house. Our son was taking a nap, and I was working in the bedroom. Daniel had gone outside to cut a piece of wood with a table saw. Within minutes I heard a scream that seemed to stop my heart! I ran outside, my husband was running, screaming, and holding an arm full of blood. He was disoriented and didn't know what to do. I immediately grab him and sat him down, then lifted his arm high to try and slow the bleeding down. I was about to put him in the car, so I could get Mathias from his nap, and rush him to the hospital. My mom and dad and two of my siblings live on the same property. I began to scream for help but then I remembered everyone was gone.

Bonetta Holloway

My uncle and aunt lived on the other side of the property. When they heard the screaming, they came running to see what had happened. Uncle Paul and I put Daniel in the car, so he could rush him to the hospital, while I got Mathias up from his nap to meet them there. Just then I heard Daniel call out to me, "Don't leave my finger! Find my finger!" The saw had cut off his index finger at the knuckle. My aunt and I started looking for it as quickly as we could. I had a million things running thru my mind, I was so overwhelmed. I finally stopped and took a breath.

It felt like the first one since I heard the scream. I was shaking so badly but I remember hearing Aunt Bama say, "Calm down baby girl it's going to be okay!" We began to brush our hands through the grass and search for the finger. There it was! Lying on the ground about fifteen feet from where he was standing, when the accident happened. I quickly ran into the house, grabbed a Ziplock bag with ice, and put his finger in it. Then quickly ran into the house to get Mathias and we rushed to the hospital. As I arrived at the little Hospital in town, they were prepping him to be moved to UBA in Birmingham. At this point I knew he was going to be ok!

As we arrived at UBA, they told us it was only a 50/50 chance that the finger would take, or that the thumb could be used again, but it was the chance Daniel wanted to take. After 10 hours of surgery, we had hope. The doctor said, "I have never seen a finger cut off at the knuckle with a saw and still have enough nerves, tissue, and meat to work with. It will take a few days of keeping a close eye on it to see if the finger and thumb will take to his hand. We had to give him a good bit of blood. He will be weak for a few days, but I have confidence, that it will take." But what scared me the most, was when the doctor said that Daniel was only about fifteen minutes from bleeding out. The fact that we lived ten minutes from the small hospital, was a blessing. All I could do was thank God.

My sisters, mom, and sisters-in-law stepped up and helped us so much during this trying time. They were faithful to keep Mathias so I could be at the hospital with Daniel. They blessed us with monetary blessing as well. When he came out of surgery, he had a big yellow foam block on his arm that looked like cheese. It had pins sticking out of his finger and thumb. The pins went all the way through to the wrist, to hold the finger and thumb in place. Daniel was dealing with the most pain he had ever experienced. Over the next four days we kept a close watch on his fingers.

The doctor would always take pictures and go on about how it was the best job he had ever seen; he would send the pictures to other doctors. This gave Daniel confidence that the doctor truly had faith that it was going to be ok. The hospital staff told us that we hit the jackpot when we got the doctor we had. They said he was one of the top 5 in his field. Trying to balance everything over the next few days was difficult. I was trying to spend as much time with Daniel as I could at the hospital, then I would drive an hour and a half home every other night to see our son. When I was home, it was hard to get any sleep. When I would lie down and it was quiet, all I could hear was the scream that Daniel let out when the saw cut him. I hated leaving him for any amount of time, he always says I am like a momma bear, but I wanted to be there if he needed me.

After six days, they sent us home with strict instructions, not to let anything touch bump or hit his fingers, or they would fall off. That made me want to stay at the hospital for a few more weeks. Just to be on the safe side! They told me I had to keep his bandages changed and help him with most of the things he did.

He could not get the hand wet or use it in anyway. The next three months was some of the hardest for him. It hurt me to see him in that kind of pain. All I could do was to be there for him, and that is what I did. I remember someone asking me if I got tired of taking care of him. I didn't understand why they were asking because he is my best friend. The one God gave me and the one who has been by my side no matter what. And when I was going through my pregnancy, he was faithful to take care of me. So, I am honored to be here for my husband and do whatever I can because I love him!

After four weeks they removed the pins out of his thumb. It was four weeks later before they took the pins out of his finger. Looking back, I still don't know how we made it through, financially. He was only receiving $250 a week from his job, but we never went without. When we had a need, the Lord would always lay it on someone's heart to help us. And I would work here and there making a little bit of money. We will never forget all those times God worked everything out right at the last minute. There was one time in particular when we had a bill due on Monday. Sunday night as we were getting ready for church, Daniel asked, "What are we going to do about this bill?" I told him, "The only thing I know, is to trust God and let Him work it out for us." Daniel said, "Yes, that is the best thing we could do." Sunday night at the end of service while in the nursery with Mathias, a pastor friend and his wife walked up and handed me a card. She hugged me and said that they felt led to give this to us. I thanked them and they left. I opened the card, and it was exactly what we needed to pay the bills the next morning! As I sat there, all I could do was cry and thank

God for coming thru yet again. That year taught us to trust God in a way we had never had too before. And ever ever since then no matter what happens in our life we just pray.

We encouraged each other that it will all work out and that Gods got it under control. A lot of times especially when there is nothing and no one in the world that can help you, you may want to lose hope. But the past few years with money, with our health, and other things we have faced, we have learned to trust in God no matter what. Sometimes it's not easy, but God has never failed us. He's never given me a reason to doubt him. I am going to trust him with everything, from the biggest problem all the way down to the smallest issue.

It was almost a year before Daniel had all the pins removed, then there was therapy and a few other small surgeries, but he did get a lot of function back in his fingers and was able to return to work. It was definitely the Lord that made it all possible! It was one of the hardest battles in our lives. Some thought it had happened because we were out of God's will. Nonetheless, through all the pain and hurting, God showed us and taught us so many things and helped us grow in so many areas of our lives.

When it first happened, we did not understand why. Looking back, we see God had His hand in it the whole time. I'm so glad He sees the things we don't.

25 | JOSH & LEANNA OUR LOVE STORY

JOSH'S STORY

Imagine yourself as a living house, and God comes in to rebuild that house. At first perhaps you can understand what He is doing. He is getting the drains right and stopping the leaks in the roof, and so on. You know those jobs needed to be done and so you are not surprised.

But presently He starts knocking the house about in a way that hurts abominably and does not seem to make any sense. What on earth is He up to? The expectation is that He is building quite a different house from the one you thought. He starts throwing out a new wing here, putting extra floor there, then running up towers and making courtyards. You thought you were being made into a decent little cottage, but he is building a palace that he intends to come and live in himself. Written by C. S. Lewis, mere Christianity

My name is Joshua Steven Holloway, I am the youngest of my five siblings. My mother the author of this book, ask if I would share a memorable life experience. As you read, I hope you will be encouraged and come to see through my story that God really does work all things together for our good. I often say to my wife, "I am nothing without you." I firmly believe God created her just for me and I for her. Even though it was a short time between us meeting and getting married. God had a plan in place. My wife says and I quote, "God had a special way of letting the two of us know we had found our soul mate. All the butterfly feelings, dates, and gifts aside, I just knew beyond the shadow of a doubt that it was you. When I prayed about our relationship there was a peace that went beyond the questions I still had about; well, everything."

My wife was attending a Bible School in Missouri when we first met, along with my cousin Makayla Swinnea, who initially introduced us. In my wife's words she shares, " I remember lying on the dorm floor writing a paper for one of my classes. And as girls do, we were talking about clothes, coffee, and how broke we were. I then said we need Mr. Tall Dark and Handsome to bring us some Takis chips, Dr. pepper, taco's and maybe a caramel frappe. Just then Makayla shoved her phone in my face and said, 'You should call my cousin Joshua.' With just one look at his picture and I was definitely interested, and willing to give this guy a chance."

Joshua, "Makayla exclaimed, "I have found the girl for you. She is sweet, smart, and single." After she presently kept calling week after week, I took her phone number, and eventually gave her a call. Through our conversation we learned a lot about each other, then soon became best friends. Then in February I felt we had a connection and I wanted to meet her face to face. So, with her father's permission, I drove all night and arrived in Missouri with plans to take her out on a date and ask her to be my girlfriend. It just happened to be Valentine's weekend, so it was perfect timing. They were taking a short break from school, which gave me a chance to hang around for a couple of days. I was permitted to stay in the boy's dorm, but I spent as much time with

Leanna as I possibly could.

My parents were a bit skeptical about me meeting a girl over the phone, and really didn't want me to drive twelve hours to meet her. They encouraged me to pray about it for a while. The week that I had planned to go we were in revival at our church with the Mullins family from Texas. During this revival I had really been praying about my future. One night as I was standing in front of the altar with my hands raised, I had been there an hour or so and desperate for direction in my life. When all of a sudden, I felt the urge to run, I started across the front of the church and I fell out in the Spirit, while I was on the floor, God affirmed to me that Leanna would be my wife. I barely knew her, but in my spirit, I knew we were going to be together in the near future.

After the service mom was cooking for the Evangelist and his family. I went into the kitchen to share with her, how that while I was lying on the floor, the Spirit let me know that not only would I meet her but one day I would marry her. Mom later told me that she was nervous about the whole thing, but she knew God had visited me on the floor that night, so, she was willing to support my decision.

LEANNA'S STORY

From my wife's point of view, "I remember the first time that Josh and I officially met. Class was just over and as I was making my way down the stairs into the school lobby, he caught me by surprise. I knew he was coming but wasn't expecting him until later that afternoon. There he was in the lobby looking straight at me. I stopped mid-stairs, and so did my heart. It was then I realized that he was truly interested in me, because he was willing to drive that great distance just to meet me. Our eyes had only connected for a millisecond, then I slipped behind the wall of the stairs so he could not see me. The anxiety soon left, and we were hanging at the local coffee shop and talking like we had known each other our whole lives. That was quite a contrast for Josh and me, we can both be a little socially awkward at times. And it still amazes me how we connected as friends so quickly. Even though we both had just came out of a serious relationship, it didn't compare to that moment we first laid eyes on each other. I am thankful that God brought our relationship at the time I most needed it in my life."

JOSH'S STORY

Leanna soon became more than a friend on April 24, 2019, my parents, and siblings all welcomed Leanna into our family. And my best friend became my bride, so now we will be forever best friends. Even though it's only been three short years, I have learned that marriage is a lot of work. A family is definitely worth having and it is worth all of the work that goes into it. Our goal is to serve the Lord and be a blessing to others.

Neither of us had any idea of how our life would be, but God ultimately had a plan. Every day we are learning to trust God, and even when we don't understand, its ok. Leanna and I have determined to let God build our home, and I believe that He will bless it with His faithfulness and eternal love.

26| 'BRO. STEVE McQUISTION

In the early 80's, Phillip and I spent a lot of time in south Louisiana. There we met a lot of wonderful people. I want to share a story about one young man in particular, named Steve McQuiston. He who was born and raised in the little town Bayou Sorrell.

When Steve was in his early twenties, he was saved in a little Baptist church there in Bayou Sorrell. He had a love for God but was too bashful to express it. He also had a great desire to work for the Lord, but never told anyone and decided to hide himself on the pew of that wonderful little Baptist church. One day Steve met a beautiful young Cajun girl, her name was Ophema Higgins. Ophema had dark brown eyes, black hair, and a beautiful smile that instantly captivated Steve. She was also the daughter of Jesse and Annie Higgins, from Jeanerette, Louisiana. Jesse and Annie were of the Pentecostal faith and in the 70's the Pentecostals were pretty emotional.

Steve wanted to date Ophema, but she would only allow him to escort her to the little Pentecostal church that she grew up in. Back in those days the preachers had strict teachings about marrying outside of your faith. So, Ophema knew Steve would have to join her church or it would never be permitted. She was dedicated to her Pentecostal belief as well and never wanted to leave her faith for nothing or no one. Steve was so bashful and a little afraid of the old-time preachers, but because he loved Ophema so much he would escort her to the revival meetings. It never failed, every time he would go, one of those fired up Pentecostal preachers would lay hands on him and tell him he was called to preach. Everyone who knew Steve doubted the fact that he could be called to preach, because he was so bashful. More and more Steve would attend church only to spend time with Ophema. Finally, Steve got what he had worked so hard for, and he and Ophema were married. He was faithful to go to church with her but sat very quietly on the pew, with his arm over the back of the pew and slightly bent onto Ophema's shoulder. Never making a sound or getting involved in any way.

In 1983, the Pastor at the church there on Higgin's Hill had become ill and had to resign the church. They ask Phillip and I to come and fill in and pray about taken the full time Pastor's position. Phillip was honored to be able to minister there for more than a year, and even though we wanted to settle there and pastor those wonderful people. Phillip was an Evangelist at heart. He never felt that he could Pastor full time. Many times, Phillip would point at Steve and say to the congregation, "You have a Pastor, you just have to wait until he is filled with the Holy Ghost." Steve was a commercial fisherman by trade. He would get out on the water in the early morning hours, make his catch and be home by noon.

After a few years of marriage and going to the Pentecostal church with his wife, he began to desire the Holy Ghost. Before leaving for work, he would go to the big house (it was the house on Higgin's Hill were the Higgin's kids were raised). No one lived there any more so, he would be there at 4 a.m. every morning and pray for an hour. He continued these early morning prayer meetings for several months. One day on his way home from fishing, as he was crossing the Morgan City bridge, with his mind on God and desiring the Holy Ghost, he began to speak in tongues. God filled him with the Holy Ghost right on top of the Morgan city bridge.

He said that he was so caught up in the spirit that he didn't remember the rest of the drive home. Steve continued with those prayer meetings and was constantly reading his bible and talking about the Lord.

His bashfulness soon began to fade as his desire for the Lord overcame it. Soon when he would go to church he would stand and ask if he could testify. Ophema was astonished, but at the same time overjoyed, because of the changed she saw in Steve. Ophema had a wonderful talent to sing, and she also played the Accordion. Every time she began to drive the billows on her Accordion and sing, under the anointing of the Holy Ghost, the blessings of the Lord would fall.

Phillip and I had been out on the road Evangelizing for quite some time, we heard reports that Brother Steve had been filled with the Holy Ghost and was starting to testify. Finally, Phillip and I were excited to learn that we were going to be attending the same camp meeting as Steve and Ophema. It was in a little church called Happy Hollow in Lake Cove, Louisiana, with Pastor David Messer. The very first night of the meeting Pastor David asked Ophema to sing. I must say we were all a bit surprise, when Steve walked to the front with her. With great boldness, Steve took the microphone and began to testify. It wasn't but a minute and he was preaching, just like those old time Pentecostal preachers he used to be afraid of. Phillip and I sat there in amazement, at how God took a young man too bashful to even talk and made him a fireball preacher.

Steve began to preach in some of the local Pentecostal churches around his hometown. People who knew him before he received the Holy Ghost, would come just to see if what they heard about Steve was true. It wasn't long until he was Evangelizing all over. Steve and Ophema had a powerful ministry. He began to sing with her, and together there singing, and preaching became well known. Two of their signature songs were "There Ain't No Grave Gonna Hold My Body Down" and "King Jesus."

After Steve had Evangelized a few years, the church on Higgin's hill in Jeanerette, Louisiana voted Steve and Ophema as their new pastors. Steve and Ophema Pastored Victory Tabernacle, there on Higgin's Hill, for many years. They moved a few miles down the road and built a brand-new building and made it the new home for Victory Tabernacle. Steve also became deeply involved in mission work.

I would like to encourage you; if you know someone who has a call on their life, don't limit God. He can make any disability vanish. Pastor Steve McQuiston recently went to heaven to gain his reward. He will forever be remembered as a Man of God, who had a passion and love for people.

Ophema was the love of his life until the day he died. She stayed true to the vows that she made to him when she was just a young girl: 'to love and to hold, for rich or for poor, in sickness and in health till death do you part.'

27| THE HOUSTON REVIVAL
SATAN SAID, "THIS IS MY PALACE"

During the early 80's we were evangelizing full time, traveling from town to town, and church to church. Those revival memories were the best. At this time, Shelly was our only child.

One of our favorite places to preach was Houston, Texas, with Pastor Henry Liles and his wife Eleanor. They were elders and treated us as if we were their own children. The church, Glory Tabernacle, sat right on the side of interstate 59 that goes right through Houston. The little church was always packed with people who loved to sing and worship the Lord. We lived in a small town so, it was exciting to go to the hustle and bustle of the big city.

The very first time we went to Houston, we pulled up to Pastor Liles' house in the little subdivision that he had lived in for many years. His back yard was fenced in, and that is where he had parked their vehicle. Phillip didn't want to intrude so he just parked on the street and pulling off into the grass, as close to the fence as he could. We went inside to visit. After about forty-five minutes, Pastor Liles jumped to his feet in a haste and said, "Where did you parked your car!" Phillip then explained, "I didn't want to intrude so I parked on the street." Pastor Liles said," We had better move it into the fence before they steal your hub caps!" Being from a small town in 1983, that never crossed our minds. As they went to move the car, sure enough, the hub caps were gone.

Just A Girl, A Journey With God

Now we understand why we saw so many little hub cap shops as we were riding through town. The next day Phillip and Pastor Liles went to the local hub cap shop and found, what was possibly, our hub caps. They were able to purchase them for a small price. We Quickly learned that we were no longer in our quite little country town. When the church service started at Glory Tabernacle it was always loud. Pastor Liles was a great singer and loved to do it for the Lord. He would sing and the people there would clap their hands and worship the Lord. Phillip would preach and then they would pray and rejoice again.

There was a lady who attended that church, her name was Sister Conn, but they called her the missionary lady. She would look for troubled young people and bring them to church. One night she brought this beautiful young girl, who was maybe seventeen years old. She was into rock and roll music, artist like AC\DC and the Kiss group. She had bracelets from her wrist to her elbow on both arms, at least ten ankle bracelets on each leg, three pierces on each ear and a thing hanging over her ear with two rings on it. She looked like a walking jewelry store.

Phillip preached and gave the altar call; everyone came to the front including this young girl. As Phillip laid hands on her she fell to the floor. As he began to pray for her, evil spirits began to leave her body one by one. Every time one would come out, she would cry and ask Phillip to help her and to not let them kill her. He assured her they would not. This went on for a couple of hours, then a man's voice spoke out of her. He said, "I am not coming out, the others were sissies, but I am the prince, and this is my palace." Phillip then said to the spirit, "You will come out in the name of Jesus because this is not your palace; it's the temple of the Holy Ghost. AND SHE BELONGS TO GOD!!"

Bonetta Holloway

After some time, the spirit did not leave. Then the Spirit of the Lord spoke to Phillip and said, "Look over your shoulder."

As he turned to look there was a man sitting there staring at him. He didn't look happy. Phillip went over to him and asked him to please come and help him pray for this young lady. He said in a gruff tone, "I will not because she does not have an evil spirit." Phillip then said to him, "Will you please walk outside until we are finished and then you can come back in." Phillip knew that his unbelief was hindering this young girl.

The man, very angrily, got up and left. We never saw him again. Shortly after the man left the spirit left that young lady. She was free that night. The next evening when she came to church, she brought three brown grocery bags. One, full of jewelry, one full of cassette tapes of her rock and roll artis, and the other full of pictures of the rock and roll groups. Pastor Liles asked Phillip what he wanted to do with them. Phillip said, "I preached over them last night, I'm not doing it again tonight." Pastor Liles suggested that they take them outside and burn them. So, there we were, right on the side of Interstate 59 in Houston Texas, engaging in an old fashion Pentecostal burning. That young lady attended the rest of that revival and God filled her with the Holy Ghost.

Several years later we saw Sister Conn the missionary lady. She said the young lady was happily married and still living for God. God is so good!

28 | DADDY, RAISED FROM THE DEAD

Willard Phillip's Dad was the manager of the cotton gin in Lecompte, Louisiana. During the off season, he would haul pulpwood. Phillip was a young boy and would often help his dad. The pulpwood had to be exactly 5 ft. 2 in. Phillip's job was to lay the measuring pole on the log. His dad would then cut the log making it the appropriate size. It was 1971, and just a week before Christmas. Phillip and his four siblings were excited, and just waiting for Christmas morning. Little did this family know, it would be a Christmas in need of a miracle.

After cutting pulp wood all day, Willard decided he would get one more load before dark. Phillip went along with his dad as he so often did. It was starting to get late but to finish up for the day, Willard decided to cut down just one more tree. In doing so, he was not aware that, as the tree fell it bent over a small sapling. Phillip put the measuring pole in place and Willard began to cut into the big tree. When he did, he also cut through the sapling that was lodged underneath. The sapling then came up with force and slapped Willard in the face, sending him backwards about five feet. Thankfully it did not knock him unconscious because Phillip was too young to drive. Willard had to drive himself out of the woods. It broke his jawbone, knocked his teeth out, and crushed his nose. It also severed the main artery in his nose, and he was bleeding profusely.

He soon arrived home with his broken bleeding nose and

teeth missing. He was quite a sight. His wife desperate to get the bleeding under control, took him to the little town clinic instead of the big hospital fifteen miles away. The doctor at the clinic did not realize his critical condition. He packed his nose with gauze's and sent him home with orders to stay in bed. With a broken jaw and teeth missing, naturally, he was not able to eat anything. With all the loss of blood, he was getting weaker by the day.

As word of his accident spread, preachers came from all over to pray for him. Pastor J. C. Swinnea, a minister of faith would often come by. As he would walk in the house, he would say, "Mildred, everything is going to be alright." His hopeful countenance and prayer of faith encouraged Mildred to keep believing for a miracle. After a few days they took Willard back to the clinic hoping to remove the gauze's and hear a good report from the doctor. But when the doctor removed the gauzes, the bleeding started again. There was not an ambulance there at the little town clinic. With no time to waste, the doctor told Mildred to get him to Saint Frances Cabrini Hospital as fast as possible. Janet, Mildred's sister was with her. Janet drove while Mildred held a pan under Willard's nose catching the blood as it poured out.

Upon arrival the doctors quickly began to try to stop the bleeding. They were never successful at completely stopping it, but they did manage to slow it down. In those days the blood banks were a little different from today. When someone in Willard's condition needed blood, on a continual basis, they would ask for people to come and donate blood for him. A friend of Willard's went around the community and found people with Willard's blood type and had them give blood. They were all so faithful taking turns and giving their blood as often as possible.

He was in ICU for days. Mildred, being the faithful wife she was, never left his side. It was a trying time for the family for sure. Mildred's mother Lena moved into their home to take care of the five children while they were in this crisis. One day the doctor was trying to give Willard blood when his veins collapsed. Mildred knew something was wrong when a rush of nurses came running in. She heard the alarm, code blue! After what seemed an eternity, the doctor looked at her and said, "I'm sorry Mrs. Holloway but his veins have collapsed and there is no more that we can do." They covered him with a sheet and told her she had to leave the room.

She replied, "Doctor I'm not leaving until I call the church and prayer is made!" Seeing the determination in her face, and feeling her grief, he graciously agreed. The doctor and nurses immediately just walked out leaving the machines connected, just to give her a moment alone. Mildred went over to the nurse's station and used the phone to call her pastor. She asked him to call everyone he could and have them pray. Mildred, being the woman of prayer that she was, never hesitated. When she hung up the phone she began to call out to God. She was not ashamed to get loud and desperate. After only a short time in prayer, the doctor and a host of nurses came running back in. Mildred, still caught up in prayer and not realizing what was going on kept praying. The doctor then pushed her out of the way and began to work with him.

His heart had started beating. They tried, once again, to give him blood. Sure enough it was successful this time. From that day he began to heal. Only a few days later, he was home. It was no doubt a miracle! Eight years later, God called Willard to preach. One day in prayer the Lord spoke to him, in a quite still voice in his heart. He said, "Move to Mellow Valley, Alabama and pioneer a church." It was his hometown. His dad had passed away when Willard was only eight months old. His mother, looking for work moved to Louisiana. Willard grew up there, and Married Mildred and raised five children. Now the Lord is sending him back home to pioneer a church. He and Mildred and their youngest son Paul, who was sixteen at the time, packed up and moved. They pastored in the little town of Mellow Valley for twenty-six years. Willard lived thirty-four years after his accident.

It is such an honor to be a part of their family. Willard and Mildred were two of the sweetest people. They always treated me like I was one of their own children. If I have learned anything at all from them, it was to be a better Christian. And that no matter what is going wrong in my life, I can! pray my way out.

29| GOD SAID, "LET GO"

When Ida turned eighteen, her dad bought her a little black Honda car. Though it was an older model and needed some work, Ida was very proud of it. But this little car was special; it had a unique problem. We bought it in the summertime, so Phillip did some minor repairs, and the little car was running fine. Well, in the early fall we went to Louisiana for a camp meeting. Ida wanted to follow us in her car to show it off, of course. When we got there, we rented our hotel room and settled in for the night. The next morning, we got up to find that a cold front had blown in during the night. Ida got in her little car to drive to the morning service, and it would not crank. Every day, Phillip would work on it trying to find the problem with no success. Soon the camp meeting was over. We had to leave her car behind with plans to come back later and get it.

Brother Chris Juneaux lived near the hotel, and he had a trailer. He told Phillip he would bring the car to his house, until we could retrieve it. Well, by the time Brother Chris went to get the car from the hotel, the weather was warm again. Out of curiosity, Chris thought to himself, "I am going to try to crank this car." And sure enough, it did crank. He drove it home with no problems. Later we discovered that every time the temperature dropped below fifty degrees, the car wouldn't crank. Well, Phillip never did find out what the problem was; it was definitely a summer car.

After a few weeks, Phillip and I went to retrieve the car. Joshua, our baby, was seven years old at the time and wanted to tag along. After a nine-hour drive, we finally made it to Brother Juneaux house. The next morning as we started out on our journey home.

Phillip decided he would drive the Honda. Just in case there was an issue with it. Joshua and I took the Suburban. We were going down interstate 10, the traffic was bumper to bumper. Phillip was in front of me; were in the left lane traveling seventy-five miles an hour, passing a few cars. We were just about to pass a man, who was in the right lane, pulling a trailer with an old lawn mower on it. Phillip had just passed him, and I was a little behind him. Just then, the big metal hood of the lawn mower flew off and began to slide right towards my vehicle. I quickly hit the shoulder, to avoid hitting the object that was flying towards me. My left tire went onto the grass, and as I was trying to get it back on the shoulder of the road, I over corrected and lost control. Phillip was watching the whole thing in his rear-view mirror and began to pray.

My vehicle was weaving from lane to lane. It seemed everything I tried only made it worse. At this point, I could feel the tires leaving the road, as it weaved from side to side. I knew it had gone too far, and we were about to flip. When I was a young girl, my sister, Theresa, decided to teach me to drive. She would always give me strict instruction that if something went wrong, she would give the word, and I was to take my hands off the wheel and put them to my side. Over the years, I would often think about those driving lessons, I can still hear my sister saying in her stern tone, "Put your hands to your side if I tell you to."

Suddenly, during all this chaos, I felt like the world stop

turning. In a moment of time God spoke to my heart and said, "Put your hands to your side and hit the brake." Well, I am much older now than I was when my sister gave me those instructions, and I have been driving for some time. I wanted to at least feel as though I was in control. But I did exactly what God told me to do. Except I closed my eyes, I then put my hands to my side, and hit the brake.

Instantly, my vehicle came to a stop. When I opened my eyes, I was setting in the grass on the left side of the road. Both lanes of traffic had stopped, and there were no accidents at all. The traffic then resumed, and I sat there for a minute trying to regain my composure. Phillip backed down the shoulder of the road to check on me. He said, "In a half a mile there is an exit, we will get off there and you can rest until you feel that you are ready to continue." So, I pulled myself together and started towards the exit.

During this time of our life, we were in a difficult financial situation. I had tried everything I could to fix it myself. But to no avail. I felt as though we were sinking, and I couldn't do anything about it. But that day, as we continued down the interstate to the exit, I was just thanking God for keeping His hand on Joshua and me. Acknowledging the fact that He showed us great mercy that day. He Spared not only my life but our seven-year-old son's life as well. Just then, God, in such a sweet calm voice, spoke to my heart again and said, "If you will take your hands off your finances and give it to me, I will fix that too." So, again I did as He said. I stopped trying to find solutions and gave it to God. God did what He said He would do. In just a short time after this, God sent someone to help us. In no time a Miracle once again was given to us.

God is so Amazing! He is mindful of his people, even when we are undeserving of it. I knew we were in this financial situation because of our carelessness. So, it was hard to trust God to remove it. But God in his mercy, looked beyond my fault and saw my need. God is an awesome God!

30| PHILLIP, "DOWN IN HIS BACK"

When Phillip was young, he had lots of back problems. If he moved the wrong way or lifted something the wrong way, it would throw his back out. One time we were scheduled to preach a revival in Shreveport, Louisiana, with Pastors Billy and Theresa Kile. Just a week before we were to leave, he was installing some heater pipes on our wood burning heater. He turned the wrong way and threw his back out. This was the worse it had ever been. He couldn't even walk. Phillip never cancelled revival for anything, but he was praying about it this time because he couldn't stand on his feet or sit. He could only lie down. Finally, after a few days he was able to stand on his feet for a short period of time, but he couldn't straighten up, and he could barely walk. With only three days until we had to leave for the revival, Phillip needed an answer. He wanted to go, but didn't know how he could make the trip, or stand to preach after he got there.

One day, he decided to walk to the church. He was all bent over and barely moving, just sliding his feet along. It took him twenty minutes or more to get there. The church was, maybe, three hundred feet away. After he got to the church, he laid on the alter, flat on his back and prayed. He said, "God I want to go to Shreveport and preach, but I need to know that you will be with me. I can't do this on my own."

After Phillip had prayed for some time, he continued to lie there. He was still and quiet, meditating on God and His goodness. Suddenly, that still small voice spoke to Phillip's heart and said, "I want you to go. Preach on cleansing the temple. There are two people there who I want you to help. So, Phillip walked home again taking twenty minutes. He came home just like when he went up there, all bent over and in great pain. He walked in the house and told me what God said, so when it was time, we loaded up and took off to Shreveport two hours away.

Shelly and Ida were the only children we had at the time. Shelly was seven years old, and Ida was two. Phillip couldn't sit, so I had to drive. Phillip always did the driving when we went places together. He liked to be in control of the wheel. This time I am driving. Shelly and Ida were in the front seat with me, which was against the law. I put Phillip in the back seat so he could lie down. In addition to all the pain he is in, he must ride lying down in the back seat, while I am driving in downtown Shreveport. He was not a happy camper to say the least. I think his pride was hurting as much as his back was, and I think he was a little scared. When we finally arrived at the hotel in Shreveport on that Saturday night, Phillip was in unbearable pain. The next morning Phillip got in the back seat to lie down, and we headed to the church. Upon arrival, he slowly made his way from the parking lot into the building. Not being able to stand or sit made it difficult for him to be there. I felt so bad for him. Phillip has always been a strong person and able to endure hardships. It was extremely hard for me to see him this way. Finally, the opening prayer and singing was over. Pastor Billy invited him to the platform. Phillip very slowly, all bent over and leaning to the left just a little, walked to the front and took the microphone. He never acknowledges his condition at all. He acted as though nothing was wrong with him. He was leaning over onto the pulpit trying to take the pressure off of his back.

He then started exalting God and bragging on God's goodness. He was quoting scripture and just lifting up the name of the Lord. After about fifteen minutes, the anointing hit him. He kicked his right leg high into the air, and he was healed! He preached, ran, jumped, and shouted for an hour. He never again had a problem with his back after that night.

Bonetta Holloway

****

I'M NOT JUST A WOMAN

Sometimes life can get so busy that we tend to lose our identity. Of course, I know I'm a woman, but it is easy to forget that I am so much more than just a woman. God said that mankind was fearfully and wonderfully made. He never expressed that more, than when He made a woman.

God put a lot of thought into how He wanted a woman to be; He then so uniquely designed her. We have read in the bible that God saw that man needed a help mate. Thinking maybe He could use something He had already created; He considered the animals. But then he realized humanity is complex. The life they would live would sometimes be complicated. So, in his Infinite Wisdom, He decided to create something much more complex than life itself; He created a woman. It is easy to have your own definition of complex, especially those of the opposite sex. I don't think God saw it in a negative way. The word complex means consisting of many different and connected parts, or not simple.

Please understand that I am not belittling the man here. God created them with strength and the wisdom to lead and direct the home. Man was first created, and then the woman was created for the man. But this is the beauty of God's Knowledge. He knew that man, by themselves, were incomplete. The life He had laid before mankind would take two people. Two people, so different, yet with an undying desire to be together. They would need to explore their future, sometimes, in a very complex way.

The title of this book is JUST A GIRL. That is all I was when the Lord found me. Just a girl simply meaning, I had little knowledge of my identity. Of course, I knew I was of the opposite sex, but I had no idea what the long-term definition of that would intel. But it wasn't long until I became a wife, and with that a whole new world was created in front of me. Shortly after, Phillip then understood that I was fearfully and wonderfully made. I can still remember, in the early days of our marriage, how I would fall apart about something. Phillip would be so confused. To him it was only a mole hill. To me it was a mountain too high to climb on my own. I am sure he probably thought he had a broken wife, and so did I. But I soon began to realize that this was part of my DNA, and too great for me to change.

When you are a wife, you also become a part of who your husband is. You are a part of his strength and weakness, his talents, and calling. My husband is a preacher. So, I carry the title preacher's wife. Now I'm not just a woman and wife but I am a preacher's wife. This doesn't put me in a greater category than anyone else, but I do understand that my life reflects my husband's ministry. I must at all times present myself in a way that will bring a positive reflection to him. Just when I thought that my life couldn't get any more complex, I became a mother. I can still remember the overwhelming fear that I felt when reality hit me. I was barely eighteen and so insecure. I couldn't imagine becoming a successful mother. But when that sweet little girl came into our lives, it seemed I matured overnight. I instantly became a light sleeper, overprotective and constantly attending her every need. I didn't have to go to school to achieve this, it came with motherhood. It was part of my

Bonetta Holloway

DNA, my makeup.

As time went on, I then became a teacher. I did home school this sweet little girl, but that is not what I'm talking about. Our children learn from example, with that being said we are all teachers. They will become the amazing man or woman that we are by nature. I can remember setting rules for my children, and they were not at all happy about it. Thinking I wasn't making a difference in their lives, I became discouraged. It wasn't until they had children of their own, and I saw them enforcing those same rules, that I then saw the fruits of my labor.

After parenthood comes a joy so overwhelming that words cannot express, Grandchildren. There is nothing in the world that can bring a joyful proud moment like seeing your children, bare children of their own. I can so vividly remember when our first grandson was born. Aiden James Wilson, he was perfect, that tiny little boy had all of us wrapped around his finger at first sight. And finally, we were grandparents. So, now I am a grandmother. I had no idea that it came with privileges. They bring those sweet grandbabies over and leave them for a few hours. Grandpa and I spoil them rotten and send them home. I LOVE IT!! So now I know that I am not just a girl, and I am not just a woman. I am a beautiful creation of God that He has fearfully and wonderfully made. A child of God. I have hopes and dreams and the power to achieve them. I have been given the opportunity to be a wife and mother through the strength of my husband. Single handedly my husband or myself can reach our greatest potential in life. But together we can conquer anything that life brings our way. When two become one they are unstoppable.

I often stand in aww when I think about God and how he

created mankind. And I am so proud to be part of his creation, and a woman. Even though it brings many dispositions to light in us, and keeps us in what feels like a whirlwind, it is so rewarding.

Well, there are many challenges in the female's roll, girl, wife, mother, grandmother, and a host of other titles that could be tagged on us....

But I will save that for another book!

Bonetta Holloway

Just A Girl, A Journey With God

Bonetta Holloway

Bonetta Holloway grew up under the beautiful Louisiana skies. In 1980, when she was just a young girl, at the age of fifteen, she married a traveling Evangelist, named Phillip. Together, she and her husband, Phillip traveled the country preaching the gospel. In 2001, they moved to the wonderful state of Alabama, where they built and pastored a church for 20 years. They have been married for over 42 years. In those years, the Lord them blessed with six beautiful children, three boys and three girls, who are now married, and 9 wonderful grandchildren. Mrs. Holloway only true credentials are being a God-fearing Christian woman, a full- time preacher's wife, and a full-time mother and grandmother. She always tells others that even though it hasn't always been easy, but OH, the journey it has been!

She hopes that through the pages of this book you will be uplifted, encouraged, and inspired to always trust that God is with you. She tells her family: "Life is a beautiful journey, and it is filled with interesting detours, and sometimes the voyage can be rough and confusing, but always remember you are not traveling alone; God is a constant companion."